A ROOM CALLED REMEMBER

OTHER BOOKS BY FREDERICK BUECHNER

FICTION

A Long Day's Dying
The Seasons' Difference
The Return of Ansel Gibbs
The Final Beast
The Entrance to Porlock
Lion Country
Open Heart
Love Feast
Treasure Hunt
The Book of Bebb
Godric

NONFICTION

The Magnificent Defeat
The Hungering Dark
The Alphabet of Grace
Wishful Thinking: A Theological ABC
The Faces of Jesus
Telling the Truth: The Gospel as Tragedy, Comedy and Fairy Tale
Peculiar Treasures: A Biblical Who's Who
The Sacred Journey
Now and Then

A ROOM CALLED
REMEMBER

Uncollected Pieces

Frederick Buechner

1817

Harper & Row, Publishers, San Francisco

Cambridge, Hagerstown, New York, Philadelphia
London, Mexico City, São Paulo, Sydney

Designer: Jim Mennick

Library of Congress Cataloging in Publication Data

Buechner, Frederick, DATE
    A ROOM CALLED REMEMBER
    1. Presbyterian Church—Sermons.   2. Sermons, American.   3. Theology—Addresses, essays, lectures.
I. Title
BX9178.B75R66 1984   252'.051   83-48457
ISBN 0-06-061163-4

89 90 91 92 10 9 8 7

For
Huyler

Contents

Preface *ix*

1. A Room Called Remember *1*

2. Faith *13*

3. Hope *24*

4. Love *36*

5. The Two Stories *46*

6. Emmanuel *57*

7. The First Miracle *66*

8. The Things That Make for Peace *70*

9. Air for Two Voices *80*

10. A Little While *91*

11. Deliverance *104*

12. Dereliction *115*

13. Delay *127*

14. The Road Goes On *138*

15. Summons to Pilgrimage *151*

16. God and Old Scratch *158*

17. The Speaking and Writing of Words *164*

18. All's Lost—All's Found *182*

Preface

Best to be honest about it—the book is a grab bag. There are a handful of sermons preached at places like Harvard, the Pacific School of Religion, the Congregational Church of Rupert, Vermont, and one that has never been preached anywhere at all ("A Room Called Remember"); an article about Christmas ("Emmanuel") which was solicited and later turned down—for being too theological, if I remember rightly—by *The New York Times Magazine;* and a couple of essays originally published in *The New York Times Book Review,* one of them an essay on religious books called "Summons to Pilgrimage" (an attempt to say what religious books *are*) and the other ("God and Old Scratch") on some of the farther-out books popular among children in this hag-ridden age of ours. Thrown in for good measure are also a commencement address delivered at Union Theological Seminary in Richmond, Virginia ("The Road Goes On"), about, among other things, a license plate that spoke to me once with staggering eloquence; a lecture on "The Speaking and Writing of Words" first given at Bangor Seminary in Maine one mild winter morning; and a short autobiographical piece ("All's Lost—All's Found") which I wrote for *The Christian Century* in answer to the question: How has your mind changed in the last decade?

"Fugitive pieces" I suppose you could call them—fugitive both in the sense of "occasional, scattered, ephemeral," and in the more basic sense, to quote Webster, of "fleeing, as from danger." The danger, of course, is oblivion.

Do they deserve to escape it? Needless to say, that is for the reader to decide. As for me, at least they seemed worth saying at the time. I tried to speak the truth in them in the sense of being as true as I could to my own experience of truth, and to direct them as accurately as I knew how toward that longing for truth that I think is a deep part of all of us even at our most jaded. Although many of them were addressed one way or another to presumed believers, I tried never to presume too much. Even at our most believing, I think, we have our serious reservations just as even at our most unbelieving we tend to cast a wistful glance over our shoulders.

Where they tend to be repetitious, simplistic, superficial, merely rhetorical, I blush for them. Where, if at all, they have any power in them to touch for good the human heart, I can say only that in that instance I have said more than I know and done better than I am.

Rupert
Vermont

1. *A Room Called Remember*

I CHRONICLES 16:1, 7–12

And they brought in the ark of God, and set it inside the tent
which David had pitched for it; and they offered burnt offerings and peace offerings before God. . . . Then on that day
David first appointed that thanksgiving be sung to the Lord by
Asaph and his brethren: "O give thanks to the Lord, call on
his name, make known his deeds among the peoples! . . . Glory
in his holy name; let the hearts of those who seek the Lord
rejoice! Seek the Lord and his strength, seek his presence
continually! Remember the wonderful works that he has done,
the wonders he wrought, the judgments he uttered.

LUKE 23:42, 43

And he said, "Jesus, remember me when you come in your
kingly power." And he said to him, "Truly, I say to you, this
day you will be with me in Paradise."

Every once in a while, if you're like me, you have a dream
that wakes you up. Sometimes it's a bad dream—a dream in
which the shadows become so menacing that your heart
skips a beat and you come awake to the knowledge that not
even the actual darkness of night is as fearsome as the
dreamed darkness, not even the shadows without as formi-
dable as the shadows within. Sometimes it's a sad dream—a
dream sad enough to bring real tears to your sleeping eyes
so that it's your tears that you wake up by, wake up to. Or

again, if you're like me, there are dreams that take a turn so absurd that you wake laughing—as if you need to be awake to savor the full richness of the comedy. Rarest of all is the dream that wakes you with what I can only call its truth.

The path of your dream winds now this way, now that —one scene fades into another, people come and go the way they do in dreams—and then suddenly, deep out of wherever it is that dreams come from, something rises up that shakes you to your foundations. The mystery of the dream suddenly lifts like fog, and for an instant it is as if you glimpse a truth truer than any you knew that you knew if only a truth about yourself. It is too much truth for the dream to hold anyway, and the dream breaks.

Several years ago I had such a dream, and it is still extraordinarily fresh in my mind. I dreamt that I was staying in a hotel somewhere and that the room I was given was a room that I loved. I no longer have any clear picture of what the room looked like, and even in the dream itself I think it wasn't so much the way the room looked that pleased me as it was the way it made me feel. It was a room where I felt happy and at peace, where everything seemed the way it should be and everything about myself seemed the way it should be too. Then, as the dream went on, I wandered off to other places and did other things and finally, after many adventures, ended back at the same hotel again. Only this time I was given a different room which I didn't feel comfortable in at all. It seemed dark and cramped, and I felt dark and cramped in it. So I made my way down to the man at the desk and told him my problem. On my earlier visit, I said, I'd had this marvelous room which was just right for me in every way and which I'd very much like if possible to have again. The trouble,

I explained, was that I hadn't kept track of where the room was and didn't know how to find it or how to ask for it. The clerk was very understanding. He said that he knew exactly the room I meant and that I could have it again anytime I wanted it. All I had to do, he said, was ask for it by its name. So then, of course, I asked him what the name of the room was. He would be happy to tell me, he said, and then he told me. The name of the room, he said, was Remember.

Remember, he said. The name of the room I wanted was Remember. That was what woke me. It shocked me awake, and the shock of it, the dazzling unexpectedness of it, is vivid to me still. I knew it was a good dream, and I felt that in some unfathomable way it was also a true dream. The fact that I did not understand its truth did not keep it from being in some sense also a blessed dream, a healing dream, because you do not need to understand healing to be healed or know anything about blessing to be blessed. The sense of peace that filled me in that room. The knowledge that I could return to it whenever I wanted to or needed to—that was where the healing and blessing came from. And the name of the room—that was where the mystery came from; that was at the heart of the healing though I did not fully understand why. The name of the room was Remember. *Why* Remember? What was there about remembering that brought a peace so deep, a sense of well-being so complete and intense that it jolted me awake in my bed? It was a dream that seemed true not only for me but true for everybody. *What* are we to re-member—all of us? To what end and purpose are we to remember?

One way or another, we are always remembering, of

course. There is no escaping it even if we want to, or at least no escaping it for long, though God knows there are times when we try to, don't want to remember. In one sense the past is dead and gone, never to be repeated, over and done with, but in another sense, it is of course not done with at all or at least not done with us. Every person we have ever known, every place we have ever seen, everything that has ever happened to us—it all lives and breathes deep in us somewhere whether we like it or not, and sometimes it doesn't take much to bring it back to the surface in bits and pieces. A scrap of some song that was popular years ago. A book we read as a child. A stretch of road we used to travel. An old photograph, an old letter. There is no telling what trivial thing may do it, and then suddenly there it all is—something that happened to us once—and it is there not just as a picture on the wall to stand back from and gaze at but as a reality we are so much a part of still and that is still so much a part of us that we feel with something close to its original intensity and fresh-ness what it felt like, say, to fall in love at the age of sixteen, or to smell the smells and hear the sounds of a house that has long since disappeared, or to laugh till the tears ran down our cheeks with somebody who died more years ago than we can easily count or for whom, in every way that matters, we might as well have died years ago ourselves. Old failures, old hurts. Times too beautiful to tell or too terrible. Memories come at us helter-skelter and unbidden, sometimes so thick and fast that they are more than we can handle in their poignance, sometimes so sparsely that we all but cry out to remember more.

But the dream seems to say more than that, to speak of a different kind of memory and to speak of remembering in a different kind of way. The kind of memories I have been naming are memories that come and go more or less on their own and apart from any choice of ours. Things remind us, and the power is the things', not ours. The room called Remember, on the other hand, is a room we can enter whenever we like so that the power of remembering becomes our own power. Also, the kind of memories we normally have are memories that stir emotions in us that are as varied as the memories that stir them. The room called Remember, on the other hand, is a room where all emotions are caught up in and transcended by an extraordinary sense of well-being. It is the room of all rooms where we feel at home and at peace. So what do these differences point to, is the question—the difference between the haphazard memories that each day brings to us willy-nilly and the memories represented by the room in the dream?

First of all, I think, they point to remembering as much more of a conscious act of the will than it normally is for us. We are all such escape artists, you and I. We don't like to get too serious about things, especially about ourselves. When we are with other people, we are apt to talk about almost anything under the sun except for what really matters to us, except for our own lives, except for what is going on inside our own skins. We pass the time of day. We chatter. We hold each other at bay, keep our distance from each other even when God knows it is precisely each other that we desperately need.

And it is the same thing when we are alone. Let's say it is late evening and everybody else has gone away or gone to bed. The time is ripe for looking back over the day, the week, the year, and trying to figure out where we have come from and where we are going to, for sifting through the things we have done and the things we have left undone for a clue to who we are and who, for better or worse, we are becoming. But again and again we avoid the long thoughts. We turn on the television maybe. We pick up a newspaper or a book. We find some chore to do that could easily wait for the next day. We cling to the present out of wariness of the past. We cling to the surface out of fear of what lies beneath the surface. And why not, after all? We get tired. We get confused. We need such escape as we can find. But there is a deeper need yet, I think, and that is the need—not all the time, surely, but from time to time—to enter that still room within us all where the past lives on as part of the present, where the dead are alive again, where we are most alive ourselves to the long journeys of our lives with all their twistings and turnings and to where our journeys have brought us. The name of the room is Remember—the room where with patience, with charity, with quietness of heart, we remember consciously to remember the lives we have lived.

So much has happened to us all over the years. So much has happened within us and through us. We are to take time to remember what we can about it and what we dare. That's what entering the room means, I think. It means taking time to remember on purpose. It means not picking up a book for once or turning on the radio, but letting the mind journey gravely, deliberately, back through the years that have gone by but are not gone. It means a deeper, slower kind of remembering; it means remembering as a searching and finding. The room is there for all of us to enter if we choose to, and the process of entering it is not unlike the process of praying because praying too is a slow, grave journey—a search to find the truth of our own lives at their deepest and dearest, a search to understand, to hear and be heard.

"Nobody knows the trouble I've seen" goes the old spiritual, and of course nobody knows the trouble we have any of us seen—the hurt, the sadness, the bad mistakes, the crippling losses—but we know it. We are to remember it. And the happiness we have seen too— the precious times, the precious people, the moments in our lives when we were better than we know how to be. Nobody knows that either, but we know it. We are to remember it. And then, if my dream was really a true dream, we will find, beyond any feelings of joy or regret that one by one the memories give rise to, a profound and undergirding peace, a sense that in some unfathomable way all is well.

We have survived, you and I. Maybe that is at the heart of our remembering. After twenty years, forty years, sixty years or eighty, we have made it to this year, this day. We needn't have made it. There were times we never thought we would and nearly didn't. There were times we almost hoped we wouldn't, were ready to give the whole thing up. Each must speak for himself, for herself, but I can say for myself that I have seen sorrow and pain enough to turn the heart to stone. Who hasn't? Many times I have chosen the wrong road, or the right road for the wrong reason. Many times I have loved the people I love too much for either their good or mine, and others I might have loved I have missed loving and lost. I have followed too much the devices and desires of my own heart, as the old prayer goes, yet often when my heart called out to me to be brave, to be kind, to be honest, I have not followed at all.

To remember my life is to remember countless times

when I might have given up, gone under, when humanly speaking I might have gotten lost beyond the power of any to find me. But I didn't. I have not given up. And each of you, with all the memories you have and the tales you could tell, you also have not given up. You also are survivors and are here. And what does that tell us, our surviving? It tells us that weak as we are, a strength beyond our strength has pulled us through at least this far, at least to this day. Foolish as we are, a wisdom beyond our wisdom has flickered up just often enough to light us if not to the right path through the forest, at least to a path that leads forward, that is bearable. Faint of heart as we are, a love beyond our power to love has kept our hearts alive.

So in the room called Remember it is possible to find peace—the peace that comes from looking back and remembering to remember that though most of the time we failed to see it, we were never really alone. We could never have made it this far if we had had only each other to depend on because nobody knows better than we do ourselves the undependability and frailty of even the strongest of us. Who or what was with us all those years? Who or what do we have to thank for our survival? Our lucky stars? Maybe just that. Maybe we have nothing more to thank than that. Our lucky stars.

But David the king had more than that or thought he did. "O give thanks to the Lord," he cried out, "make known his deeds among the peoples!" He had brought the ark of the covenant into Jerusalem and placed it in a room, a tent, and to the sound of harp, lyre, cymbals, and trumpet he sang his wild and exultant song. "Remember the wonderful works that he has done," he sang, "the wonders he wrought, the judgments he uttered." *Remember* was the song David sang, and what memories he had or was to have, what a life to remember!—his failure as a husband and a father, his lust for Bathsheba and the murder of her husband, his crime against Naboth and the terrible denunciation of the prophet Nathan, his failures, his betrayals, his hypocrisy. But "Tell of his salvation from day to day," his song continues nonetheless and continued all his life, and I take him to mean not just that the telling was to take place from day to day but that salvation itself takes place from day to day. Every day, as David remembered, he had been somehow saved—saved enough to survive his own darkness and lostness and folly, saved enough to go on through thick and thin to the next day and the next day's saving and the next. "Remember the wonders he wrought, the judgments he uttered," David cries out in his song, and the place where he remembers these wonders and judgments is his own past in all its brokenness and the past of his people before him, of Abraham, Isaac and Jacob, the Exodus, the entrance into the Promised Land, which are all part of our past too as Christ also is part of our past, that Exodus, that Promised Land, and all those mightier wonders yet. That's what he remembers and sings out for us all to remember.

"Seek the Lord and his strength, seek his presence continually" goes the song—seek him in the room in the tent where the holy ark is, seek him in the room in the dream. It is the Lord, it is God, who has been with us through all our days and years whether we knew it or not, he sings—with us in our best moments and in our worst moments, to heal us with his wonders, to wound us healingly with his judgments, to bless us in hidden ways though more often than not we had forgotten his name.

It is God that David thanks and not his lucky stars. "O give thanks to the Lord . . . make known his deeds among the peoples," he sings; remember and make known the deeds that he wrought among the years of your own lives. Is he right? Was it God? Is it God we have to thank, you and I, for having made it somehow to this day?

Again each of us must speak for himself, for herself. We must, each one of us, remember our own lives. Someone died whom we loved and needed, and from somewhere something came to fill our emptiness and mend us where we were broken. Was it only time that mended, only the resurging busyness of life that filled our emptiness? In anger we said something once that we could have bitten our tongues out for afterwards, or in anger somebody said something to us. But out of somewhere forgiveness came, a bridge was rebuilt; or maybe forgiveness never came, and to this day we have found no bridge back. Is the human heart the only source of its own healing? Is it the human conscience only that whispers to us that in bitterness and estrangement is death? We listen to the evening news with its usual recital of shabbiness and horror, and God, if we believe in him at all, seems remote and powerless, a child's dream. But there are other times—often the most unexpected, unlikely times—when strong as life itself comes the sense that there is a holiness deeper than shabbiness and horror and at the very heart of darkness a light unutterable. Is it only the unpredictable fluctuations of the human spirit that we have to thank? We must each of us answer for ourselves, remember for ourselves, preach to ourselves our own sermons. But "Remember the wonderful works," sings King David because if we remember deeply and truly, he says, we will know whom to thank, and in that room of thanksgiving and remembering there is peace.

Then hope. Then at last we see what hope is and where it comes from, hope as the driving power and outermost edge of faith. Hope stands up to its knees in the past and keeps its eyes on the future. There has never been a time past when God wasn't with us as the strength beyond our strength, the wisdom beyond our wisdom, as whatever it is in our hearts—whether we believe in God or not—that keeps us human enough at least to get by despite everything in our lives that tends to wither the heart and make us less than human. To remember the past is to see that we are here today by grace, that we have survived as a gift.

And what does that mean about the future? What do we have to hope for, you and I? Humanly speaking, we have only the human best to hope for: that we will live out our days in something like peace and the ones we love with us; that if our best dreams are never to come true, neither at least will our worst fears; that something we find to do with our lives will make some little difference for good somewhere and that when our lives end we will be remembered a little while for the little good we did. That is our human hope. But in the room called Remember we find something beyond it.

"Remember the wonderful works that he has done," goes David's song—remember what he has done in the lives of each of us, and beyond that remember what he has done in the life of the world; remember above all what he has done in Christ—remember those moments in our own lives when with only the dullest understanding but with the sharpest longing we have glimpsed that Christ's kind of life is the only life that matters and that all other kinds of life are riddled with death; remember those moments in our lives when Christ came to us in countless disguises through people who one way or another strengthened us, comforted us, healed us, judged us, by the power of Christ alive within them. All that is the past. All that is what there is to remember. And *because* that is the past, *because* we remember, we have this high and holy hope: that what he has done, he will continue to do, that what he has begun in us and our world, he will in unimaginable ways bring to fullness and fruition.

"Let the sea roar, and all that fills it, let the field exult and everything in it! Then shall the trees of the wood sing for joy," says David. And *shall* is the verb of hope. Then death shall be no more, neither shall there be mourning or crying. Then shall my eyes behold him and not as a stranger. Then his kingdom shall come at last and his will shall be done in us and through us and for us. Then the trees of the wood shall sing for joy as already they sing a little even now sometimes when the wind is in them and as underneath their singing our own hearts too already sing a little sometimes at this holy hope we have.

The past and the future. Memory and expectation. Remember and hope. Remember and wait. Wait for him whose face we all of us know because somewhere in the past we have faintly seen it, whose life we all of us thirst for because somewhere in the past we have seen it lived, have maybe even had moments of living it ourselves. Remember him who himself remembers us as he promised to remember the thief who died beside him. To have faith is to remember and wait, and to wait in hope is to have what we hope for already begin to come true in us through our hoping. Praise him.

2. Faith

HEBREWS 11:3, 7–14 passim

By faith we understand that the world was created by the word of God, so that what is seen was made out of things which do not appear. . . . By faith Noah, being warned by God concerning events as yet unseen, took heed and constructed an ark for the saving of his household. . . . By faith Abraham . . . went out, not knowing where he was to go. . . . By faith Sarah herself received power to conceive even when she was past the age. . . . These all died in faith, not having received what was promised, but having seen it and greeted it from afar, and having acknowledged that they were strangers and exiles on the earth. For people who speak thus make it clear that they are seeking a homeland.

Every once in a while, life can be very eloquent. You go along from day to day not noticing very much, not seeing or hearing very much, and then all of a sudden, when you least expect it very often, something speaks to you with such power that it catches you off guard, makes you listen whether you want to or not. Something speaks to you out of your own life with such directness that it is as if it calls you by name and forces you to look where you have not had the heart to look before, to hear something that maybe for years you have not had the wit or the courage to hear. I was on my way home from a short trip I took not long ago when such a thing happened to me—three such things actually, three images out of my journey, that haunt me still with what seems a truth that it is important to tell.

The first thing was this. I was on a train somewhere along that grim stretch of track between New Brunswick, New Jersey, and New York City. It was a grey fall day with low clouds in the sky and a scattering of rain in the air, a day as bleak and insistent as a headache. The train windows were coated with dust, but there isn't all that much to see through them anyway except for the industrial wilderness that spreads out in all directions around you and looks more barren and more abandoned as you approach Newark—the flat, ravaged earth, the rubble, the endless factories black as soot against the sky with their tall chimneys that every now and then are capped with flame like a landscape out of Dante. I was too tired from where I'd been to feel much like reading and still too caught up in what I'd been doing to be able to doze very satisfactorily, so after gazing more or less blindly out of the dirty window for a while, I let my eyes come to rest on the nearest bright thing there was to look at, which was a large color photograph framed on the wall up at the front end of the coach.

It was a cigarette ad, and I forget what was in it exactly, but there was a pretty girl in it and a good-looking boy, and they were sitting together somewhere—by a mountain stream, maybe, or a lake, with a blue sky overhead, green trees. It was a crisp, sunlit scene full of beauty, of youth, full of *life* more than anything else, and thus as different as it could have been from the drabness I'd been looking at through the window until I felt just about equally drab inside myself. And then down in the lower left-hand corner of the picture, in letters large enough to read from where I was sitting, was the Surgeon General's familiar warning about how cigarette smoking can be hazardous to your health, or whatever the words are that they use for saying that cigarette smoking can cause lung cancer and kill you dead as a doornail.

It wasn't that I hadn't seen such ads thousands of times before and boggled at the macabre irony of them—those pretty pictures, that fatal message—but for some reason having to do with being tired, I suppose, and having nothing else much to look at or think about, I was so stunned by this one that I haven't forgotten it yet. "Buy this; it will kill you," the ad said. "Choose out of all that is loveliest and greenest and most innocent in the world that which can make you sick before your time and bring your world to an end. Live so you will die."

I'm not interested here in scoring a point against the advertising business or the tobacco industry, and the dangers of cigarette smoking are not what I want to talk about; what I want to talk about is something a great deal more dangerous still which the ad seemed to be proclaiming with terrible vividness and power. We are our own worst enemies, the ad said. That's what I want to talk about. I had heard it countless times before as all of us have, but this time the ad hit me over the head with it—that old truism that is always true, spell it out and apply it however you like. As nations we stockpile new weapons and old hostilities that may well end up by destroying us all; and as individuals we do much the same. As individuals we stockpile weapons for defending ourselves against not just the things and the people that threaten us but against the very things and people that seek to touch our hearts with healing and make us better and more human than we are. We stockpile weapons for holding each other at arm's length, for wounding sometimes even the ones who are closest to us. And as for hostilities—toward other people, toward ourselves, toward God if we happen to believe in him—we can all name them silently and privately for ourselves.

The world is its own worst enemy, the ad said. The world, in fact, is its *only* enemy. No sane person can deny it, I think, as suddenly the picture on the wall of the train jolted me into being sane and being unable to deny it myself. The pretty girl and the good-looking boy. The lake and trees in all their beauty. The blue sky in all its innocence and mystery. And, tucked in among it all, this small, grim warning that we will end by destroying ourselves if we're not lucky. We need no urging to choose what it is that will destroy us because again and again we choose it without urging. If we don't choose to smoke cigarettes ourselves, we choose at least to let such ads stand without batting an eye. "Buy this; it can kill you," the pretty picture said, and nobody on the train, least of all myself, stood up and said, "Look, this is madness!" Because we are more than half in love with our own destruction. All of us are. That is what the ad said. I suppose I had always known it, but for a moment—rattling along through the Jersey flats with the grey rain at the window and not enough energy to pretend otherwise for once—I more than knew it. I choked on it.

The second thing was not unlike the first in a way, as if, in order to put the point across, life had to hit me over the head with it twice. I haven't led an especially sheltered life as lives go. I've knocked around more or less like everybody else and have seen my share of the seamy side of things. I was born in New York City and lived there off and on for years. I've walked along West Forty-Second Street plenty of times and seen what there is to see there though I've tried not to see it—wanted to see it and tried not to see it at the same time. I've seen the double and triple X-rated movie houses catering to every kind of grotesqueness and cruelty and patheticness of lust. I've seen the adult bookstores, the peep shows, the massage parlors, and sex shops with people hanging around the doors to con you into entering. I've seen the not all that pretty girls and less than good-looking boys—many of them hardly more than children, runaways—trying to keep alive by clumsily, shiftily selling themselves for lack of anything else to sell; and staggering around in the midst of it all, or slumped like garbage against the fronts of buildings, the Forty-Second Street drunks—not amiable, comic drunks you can kid yourself into passing with a smile, but angry, bloodshot, crazy drunks, many of them blacks because blacks in New York City have more to be angry and crazy about than the rest of us.

I'd seen it all before and will doubtless see it all again, but walking from my train to the Port Authority Bus Terminal—and with that ad, I suppose, still on my mind—I saw it almost as if for the first time. And, as before, I'm not so much interested in scoring a point against the sex industry, or against the indifference or helplessness or ineptitude of city governments, or against the plague of alcoholism; because instead, again, it was the very sight I saw that scored a point against me, against our world. I found myself suddenly so scared stiff by what I saw that if I'd known a place to hide, I would have gone and hidden there. And what scared me most was not just the brutality and ugliness of it all but how vulnerable I was to the brutality and ugliness, how vulnerable to it we all of us are and how much it is a part of us.

What scared the daylights out of me was to see suddenly how drawn we all are, I think, to the very things that appall us—to see how beneath our civilizedness, our religiousness, our humanness, there is that in all of us which remains uncivilized, religionless, subhuman, and which hungers for precisely the fare that Forty-Second Street offers, which is basically the license to be subhuman not just sexually but any other way that appeals to us—the license to use and exploit and devour each other like savages, to devour and destroy our own sweet selves. And if you and I are tempted to think we don't hunger for such things, we have only to remember some of the dreams we dream and some of the secrets we keep and the battle against darkness we all of us fight. I was scared stiff that I would somehow get lost in that awful place and never find my way out. I was scared that everybody I saw coming toward me down the crowded sidewalk—old and young, well dressed and ragged, innocent and corrupt—was in danger of getting lost. I was scared that the world itself was as lost as it was mad. And of course in a thousand ways it is.

The third thing was finally getting home. It was late and dark when I got there after a long bus ride, but there were lights on in the house. My wife and daughter were there. They had waited supper for me. There was a fire in the woodstove, and the cat was asleep on his back in front of it, one paw in the air. There are problems at home for all of us—problems as dark in their way as the dark streets of any city—but they were nowhere to be seen just then. There was nothing there just then except stillness, light, peace, and the love that had brought me back again and that I found waiting for me when I got there. Forty-Second Street was only a couple of hundred miles from my door, but in another sense it was light-years away.

Part of what I felt, being home, was guilt, because feeling guilty is one of the things we all are so good at. I felt guilty about having, at home, the kind of peace which the victims and victimizers of Forty-Second Street not only don't have but don't even know exists because that is part of the price you pay for being born into the world poor, unloved, without hope. "I was hungry and you gave me food," Christ said. "I was a stranger and you welcomed me. . . . I was sick and you visited me," Christ said, and by coming home I was turning my back not just on Christ but on all the sick, the hungry, the strangers in whom Christ is present and from whom I'd fled like a bat out of hell—just that, because hell was exactly where I'd been. But I wouldn't let myself feel guilty long; I fought against feeling guilty, because as I sat there in that warm, light house, safe for the moment from the darkness of night and from all darkness, I felt something else so much more powerful and real.

Warmth. Light. Peace. Stillness. Love. That was what I felt. And as I entered that room where they were present, it seemed to me that wherever these things are found in the world, they should not be a cause for guilt but treasured, nurtured, sheltered from the darkness that threatens them. I thought of all such rooms everywhere—both rooms inside houses and rooms inside people—and how in a way they are like oases in the desert where green things can grow and there is refreshment and rest surrounded by the sandy waste; how in a way they are like the monasteries of the Dark Ages where truth, wisdom, charity were kept alive surrounded by barbarity and misrule.

The world and all of us in it are half in love with our own destruction and thus mad. The world and all of us in it are hungry to devour each other and ourselves and thus lost. That is not just a preacher's truth, a rhetorical truth, a Sunday School truth. Listen to the evening news. Watch television. Read the novels and histories and plays of our time. Read part of what there is to be read in every human face including my face and your faces. But every once in a while in the world, and every once in a while in ourselves, there is something else to read—there are places and times, inner ones and outer ones, where something like peace happens, love happens, light happens as it happened for me that night I got home. And when they happen, we should hold on to them for dear life, because of course they are dear life. They are glimpses and whispers from afar: that peace, light, love are where life ultimately comes from, that deeper down than madness and lostness they are what at its heart life is. By faith we know this, and I think only by faith, because there is no other way to know it.

"By faith we understand that the world was created by the word of God, so that what is seen was made out of things which do not appear," says the author of Hebrews. Faith is a way of looking at what is seen and understanding it in a new sense. Faith is a way of looking at what there is to be seen in the world and in ourselves and hoping, trusting, believing against all evidence to the contrary that beneath the surface we see there is vastly more that we cannot see.

What is it "that is seen," as Hebrews puts it? What is seen is the ruined landscape I saw through the train window, the earth so ravaged you can't believe any green thing will ever grow there again. What is seen is all the streets in the world like Forty-Second Street—the crazy drunks, the child whores, the stink of loneliness, emptiness, cruelty, despair. Maybe most of all what is seen, if we're honest, is that there is in all of us what is both sickened and fascinated by such things, attracted and repelled. What is seen is a world that tries to sell us what kills us like the cigarette ad and never even gives it a second thought as you and I rarely give it a second thought either but rush to buy what the world sells, and in our own way sell it ourselves.

Who or what created such a world? On the face of it, there seems to be only one answer to that question. We ourselves created it—that is the answer—and it is hard to see on the face of it—hard to *see*—that what created us can have been anything more than some great cosmic upheaval, some slow, blind process as empty of meaning or purpose as a glacier. But "by faith," says Hebrews, we see exactly the same world and yet reach exactly the opposite answer, which is faith's answer. "By faith we understand that the world was created by the word of God," it says, "so that what is seen was made out of things which do not appear."

By faith we understand, if we are to understand it at all, that the madness and lostness we see all around us and within us are not the last truth about the world but only the next to the last truth. Madness and lostness are the results of terrible blindness and tragic willfulness which whole nations are involved in no less than you and I are involved in them. Faith is the eye of the heart, and by faith we see deep down beneath the face of things—by faith we struggle against all odds to be able to see—that the world is God's creation even so. It is he who made us and not we ourselves, made us out of his peace to live in peace, out of his light to dwell in light, out of his love to be above all things loved and loving. That is the last truth about the world.

Can it be true? No, of course it cannot. On the face of it, if you take the face seriously and face up to it, how can it possibly be true? Yet how can it not be true when our own hearts bear such powerful witness to it, when blessed moments out of our own lives speak of it so eloquently? And that no-man's-land between the Yes and the No, that everyman's land, is where faith stands and has always stood. Seeing but not seeing, understanding but not understanding, we all stand somewhere between the Yes and the No the way old Noah stood there before us, and Abraham, and Sarah his wife, all of them. The truth of God as the last and deepest truth—they none of them saw it in its fullness any more than we have, but they spent their lives homesick for it—seeking it like a homeland, like home, and their story is our story because we too have seen from afar what peace is, light is, love is, and we have seen it in something like that room that love brought me back to that rainy day on the train and the bus, and where I found supper waiting, found love waiting, love enough to see me through the night.

That still, light room in that house—and whatever that

room represents of stillness and light and the possibility of faith, of Yes, in your own lives—is a room to find healing and hope in, but it is also a room with a view. It is a room which looks out, like the window of the train, on a landscape full of desolation—which looks out on Forty-Second Street with its crowds of hungry ones, lonely ones, sick ones, all the strangers who turn out not to be strangers after all because we are all of us seeking the same homeland together whether we know it or not, even the mad ones and lost ones who scare us half to death because in so many ways they are so much like ourselves.

Maybe in time we will even be able to love them a little —to feed them when they are hungry and maybe no farther away than our own street; to visit them when they are sick and lonely; maybe hardest of all, to let them come serve us when the hunger and sickness and loneliness are not theirs but ours. "Your faith has made you whole," Jesus said to the woman who touched the hem of his garment, and maybe by grace, by luck, by holding fast to whatever of him we can touch, such faith as we have will make us whole enough to become something like human at last—to see something of the power and the glory and the holiness beneath the world's lost face. That is the direction that home is in anyway—the homeland we have seen from afar in our dearest rooms and truest dreams, the homeland we have seen in the face of him who is himself our final home and haven, our kingdom and king.

3. Hope

EXODUS 3:1–6

Now Moses was keeping the sheep of his father-in-law, Jethro, the priest of Midian; and he led his flock to the west side of the wilderness, and came to Horeb, the mountain of God. And the angel of the Lord appeared to him in a flame of fire out of the midst of a bush; and he looked, and lo, the bush was burning, yet it was not consumed. And Moses said, "I will turn aside and see this great sight, why the bush is not burnt." When the Lord saw that he turned aside to see, God called to him out of the bush, "Moses, Moses!" And he said, "Here am I." Then he said, "Do not come near; put off your shoes from your feet for the place on which you are standing is holy ground." And he said, "I am the God of your father, the God of Abraham, the God of Isaac, and the God of Jacob." And Moses hid his face, for he was afraid to look at God.

LUKE 19:37–40

As he was now drawing near, at the descent of the Mount of Olives, the whole multitude of the disciples began to rejoice and praise God with a loud voice for all the mighty works that they had seen, saying, "Blessed is the King who comes in the name of the Lord! Peace in heaven and glory in the highest!" And some of the Pharisees in the multitude said to him, "Teacher, rebuke your disciples." He answered, "I tell you, if these were silent, the very stones would cry out."

It is one of the great moments in Old Testament history. Perhaps it is the key moment. Moses was a stranger and exile in a strange land—in Midian, on the east bank of the Gulf of Aquabah—the land he fled to from Egypt where he had murdered an Egyptian for beating a Hebrew slave. With death on his conscience, he had fled for his life, left everything behind. He married a Midianite woman, settled down, and was tending his father-in-law's sheep on the slopes of Mt. Horeb in the wilderness when suddenly the moment happened. A bush burst into flame. It blazed up, the heat of it rippling the air around it. Leaf and stem, it became all fire, crackling, leaping, as if the air itself was on fire. But though the bush burned, it did not burn up because it was a miraculous fire, which is to say a fire that Moses could not explain anymore than we can explain it except by explaining it away as no real fire at all but only a figment of Mose's fiery imagination or the pious invention of a later time.

Then out of the flaming moment, a voice also flamed up, and of all the conceivable things it might have said, what it said was the name of Moses himself. "Moses," it said, "Moses," twice, and at the sound of his own name he was caught, as we also would have been caught, because we so much *are* our own names that at the sound of them we cannot help listening whether we want to or not because the voice that calls us by name is a voice that knows us by name, knows *us,* and has something to say to us, and for all we know everything may depend on our listening and answering. So Moses, the stranger and exile, stood there with the muck of the sheep on his shoes, and guilty as hell of a man's murder and listened and answered.

"Here am I," he said, waiting for God only knows what to happen next, what lightning bolt to strike him on fire himself like the bush. Only what happened instead was that when the voice out of the fire spoke again, what it said was, "Put off your shoes from your feet, because the place on which you are standing is holy ground." That scrubby patch of upland wilderness that the sheep had mucked up, that patch of no-man's-land that Moses had fled to for no motive holier than to save his own skin, was holy, the voice said, because it was as aflame with God as the bush was aflame with fire. Then the voice identified itself. It was God's voice, the God of Abraham, Isaac and Jacob, the voice said. And then Moses hid his face, the Book of Exodus says, "for he was afraid to look at God," and well he might have been afraid if he had any inkling of what God was going to say next, because what God said next was as holy and fiery a word as there is in the Old Testament or anywhere else. That word was GO.

For those of us who are in the habit of putting on our best clothes and going to church from time to time, maybe it is a good idea to consider what a church is, of all things. What are all these churches we keep coming to, year in and year out? A church in the sense of a building is walls and a roof erected on the proposition that this ancient story of Moses and his burning bush is somehow true— that however you choose to explain that story, you cannot all that easily explain it away. Something extraordinary took place a long time ago on the eastern shore of the Gulf of Aquabah, and our presence in churches, and the presence of millions like us, is evidence that the reverberations of that event are felt to this day. It is the reason why churches exist. It is the reason why we go to them though we often forget it and go for shabbier reasons. The old church walls, the old church roofs, were put up in the faith that if God is present anywhere in the world, he is present everywhere, and that if the ground that Moses stood on was holy, then the little patches of ground where churches stand are holy too. The whole earth is holy because God makes himself known on it, which means that in that sense a church is no holier than any other place. God is not more in a church than he is anywhere else. But what makes a church holy in a special way is that we ourselves are more here.

What I mean is that if we come to a church right, we come to it more fully and nakedly ourselves, come with more of our humanness showing, than we are apt to come to most places. We come like Moses with muck on our shoes—footsore and travel-stained with the dust of our lives upon us, our failures, our deceits, our hypocrisies, because if, unlike Moses, we have never taken anybody's life, we have again and again withheld from other people, including often even those who are nearest to us, the love that might have made their lives worth living, not to mention our own. Like Moses we come here as we are, and like him we come as strangers and exiles in our way because wherever it is that we truly belong, whatever it is that is truly home for us, we know in our hearts that we have somehow lost it and gotten lost. Something is missing from our lives that we cannot even name—something we know best from the empty place inside us all where it belongs. We come here to find what we have lost. We come here to acknowledge that in terms of the best we could be we are lost and that we are helpless to save ourselves. We come here to confess our sins.

That is the sadness and searching of what a church is, of what we are in a church—and then suddenly FIRE! The bush bursts into flame. And the voice speaks our names, whatever they are—Peter, John, Ann, Mary. The heart skips a beat. YOU! YOU! the voice says. Does it? Does any voice other than a human voice speak in this place? Does any flame other than candle flame on Christmas Eve ever leap here? I think so. I think if you have your ears open, if you have your eyes open, every once in a while some word in even the most unpromising sermon will flame out, some scrap of prayer or anthem, some moment of silence even, the sudden glimpse of somebody you love sitting there near you, or of some stranger whose face without warning touches your heart, will flame out—and these are the moments that speak our names in a way we cannot help hearing. These are the moments that in the depths of whatever our dimness and sadness and lostness are, give us an echo of a wild and bidding voice that calls us from deeper still. It is the same voice that Moses heard and that one way or another says GO! BE! LIVE! LOVE! sending us off on an extraordinary and fateful journey for which there are no sure maps and whose end we will never fully know until we get there. And for as long as the moment lasts, we suspect that maybe it is true—maybe the ground on which we stand really is holy ground because we heard that voice here. It called us by name.

Is it madness to believe such a thing? That is a serious question. Is it madness to believe in God at all let alone in a God who speaks to us through such obscure and fleeting moments as these and then asks us to believe that these moments are windows into the truest meaning and mystery of the cosmos itself? It is a kind of madness indeed. A famous scientist recently gave a definitive answer as to what the cosmos is. "The cosmos," he said, "is all there is or ever was or ever will be." Which means that if you want to understand the cosmos, there is nothing other than the cosmos itself that you can look to for your answer.

Where did the world come from and where is it going? Ask the geologists and cosmologists, such a man would say. Ask the astrophysicists, the philosophers even. They may not have all the answers today, but as government puts more money into research, and as technology becomes more sophisticated, they will have them tomorrow. What is the human being? The advances in biology, biochemistry, genetics, over the last few years have been extraordinary, and such problems as the structure of the brain, the nature of disease, the chemical origins and make-up of life itself come closer to a solution every day. Or maybe your questions are more practical than theoretical. How do we get on in this world with the bodies and brains that we have? How do we stay healthy, cure cancer? How do we cope with the psychological tensions of modern living? How do we keep our heads above water economically, environmentally? What about the arms race, the tens of thousands dying of starvation in Africa? What about the failed marriage? The suicidal eighteen-year-old?

There are times for all of us when life seems without purpose or meaning, when we wake to a sense of chaos like a great cat with its paws on our chests sucking our breath. What can we do? Where can we turn? Well, you can thank your lucky stars, say many among us, that the world is full of specialists who are working on all these problems; and you can turn to them, men and women who have put behind them all the ancient myths and dreams and superstitions and have dedicated themselves to finding solutions to these problems in the only place where solutions or anything else can be found—which is here in the midst of the vast complexities of the cosmos itself, which is all there is or ever was or ever will be.

The existence of the church bears witness to the belief that there is only one thing you can say to such a view and that is that it is wrong. There is only one answer you can give to this terrible sanity, and that is that it is ultimately insane. The ancient myths and dreams of a power beyond power and a love beyond love that hold the cosmos itself, hold all things, in existence reflect a reality which we can deny only to our great impoverishment; and the dream of a holiness and mystery at the heart of things that humankind with all its ingenuity and wisdom can neither explain away nor live fully without goes on being dreamed. Moments continue to go up in flames like the bush in Midian to illumine, if only for a moment, a path that stretches before us like no other path. And such moments call out in a voice which, if we only had courage and heart enough, we would follow to the end of time.

For a human being to say that the cosmos is all there is strikes me as like a worm in an apple saying that the apple is all there is. Even if we could solve all the problems of the cosmos and stood here healthy, solvent, adjusted, and proud in our knowledge at last, we would still stand here like Moses with the muck of our less-than-humanness on our shoes and the feeling in the pits of our stomachs that the cosmos can never entirely be home because we know as surely as we know anything that though we have never seen it except in dreams, our true home lies somewhere else. Those dreams are the ultimate madness the church is built upon, or, because those who call them madness are themselves madder still, the ultimate sanity.

But enough of all that. We have come to this church, and for centuries others like us have come to church too, so it is to them we should turn our attention, the people who came here over the years and why they came and what they found when they got here or failed to find. People came to this church for the same reasons they came to any church anywhere, and my guess is that many of their reasons were just about as inconsequential as many of ours. They came because there wasn't all that much else to do on Sundays and there was no nine-thousand-page *New York Times* to drowse over. They came to see their friends and be seen by them. They came out of habit because they had always come, and out of tradition because their ancestors had come before them. They came to be entertained, maybe even to be edified. They came, even the ones who in their secret hearts believed very little, with the idea that just maybe there is a God who keeps track of who comes and who doesn't and it is just as well to stay on his good side. Sometimes they enjoyed themselves here, and sometimes they were bored stiff. Sometimes they were set to thinking long thoughts about themselves and their lives, but as often as not their minds probably wandered off into the same anxieties, fantasies, daydreams that they would have lost themselves in if they had been riding the bus or waiting their turn at the dentist. And in all of this, their ministers were probably not all that different. Sometimes their hearts were in it, and sometimes it was just a job to get done, a sermon to be preached, a collection to take.

Ministers and congregation both, they came to church year after year, and who is to say how if at all their lives were changed as the result? If you'd stopped and asked them on any given Sunday, I suspect they would have said they weren't changed much. Yet they kept on coming anyway; and beneath all the lesser reasons they had for doing so, so far beneath that they themselves were only half aware of it, I think there was a deep reason, and if I could give only one word to characterize that reason, the word I would give is *hope.*

They came here, the awkward boys and shy girls, to get married and stood here with their hearts in their mouths and their knees knocking to mumble their wild and improbable vows in these very shadows. They came to christen their babies here—carried them in in their long white dresses hoping they wouldn't scream bloody. murder when the minister took them in his arms and signed their foreheads with a watery cross. They came here to bury their dead, and brought in, along with the still, finished bodies, all the most un-still, unfinished love, guilt, sadness, relief, that are part of what death always is for the living. In other words what they were doing essentially beneath this roof was offering up the most precious moments of their lives in the hope that there was a God to hallow them—a God to hear and seal their vows, to receive their children into his unimaginable kingdom, to raise up and cherish their dead. I see them sitting here, generations of them, a little uncomfortable in their Sunday best with their old faces closed like doors and their young faces blank as clapboard; but deep within those faces— farther down than their daydreams and boredom and way beyond any horizon of their wandering minds that they could describe—there was the hope that somewhere out of all the words and music and silences of this place, and out of a mystery even greater than the mystery of the cosmos itself, a voice that they would know from all other voices would speak their names and bless them.

I think also of a school church where I served once as chaplain. People didn't get married and christened there very much and death rarely entered because that wasn't the kind of church it was. The people in the pews weren't townspeople—the rich men, poor men, beggarmen, thieves of that town—but teenage boys, hundreds of them, all shapes and all sizes, from all over the map and from every sort of religious background or no religious background at all. They came because they knew they would catch bloody hell from the Dean's office if they didn't. So come they did, pulling up their ties and choking down their breakfasts as they raced through drifts of autumn leaves or snow to get in before the last stroke of the last bell sounded. And what many of them brought with them was their hostility to religion in general and church in particular, their skepticism about the whole business of God, their determination, many of them, not to look interested even if they were, all of which means that in many ways they weren't as different from you and me as at first glance it might appear because there is something in all of us that is full of doubts about religion and church and God himself, full of skepticism and hostility.

And what did they find when they got there? They didn't find ministers who had known them and their families for years but a succession of visiting preachers, many of them the great ones of their time, who preached the Gospel with all the wit and eloquence they could muster in the name not only of Almighty God but of the school itself in the person of the Principal who sat up there on the platform with them like a lion under the throne. And for nine years they also found me there—the new school minister, young and green in his job, having never ministered to anybody before let alone to such a three-ring circus as that. So I did what I could, and what I could was to try like the others to set forth such faith as I had with all the power I could muster.

I had the feeling that for many of the boys who went there, this was the last time they would be so much as caught dead in a church ever again, which meant that this was just possibly the last chance anybody might ever have to speak to them seriously about Christ and about what life with Christ involves and what life without Christ involves too. So for nine years I ran scared and never climbed into that pulpit without my mouth going dry and my stomach in a turmoil at the sense I had of the terrible urgency of what I was about. There they would be, Sunday after Sunday, sitting in their seats much as you are sitting in yours and not wanting, most of them, to be there at all, and showing it. But as I looked out at their faces the way I look out now at yours, I had again and again the uncanny sense that from time to time, in spite of themselves, they were truly listening.

Different as that school church was from churches in general, and different as those boys were from you and me, I think that what lay at the heart of their listening was the same thing that lies no less at your heart and mine and at the hearts of all the generations who worshiped here before us. I think it is hope that lies at our hearts and hope that finally brings us all here. Hope that in spite of all the devastating evidence to the contrary, the ground we stand on is holy ground because Christ walked here and walks here still. Hope that we are known, each one of us, by name, and that out of the burning moments of our lives he will call us by our names to the lives he would have us live and the selves he would have us become. Hope that into the secret grief and pain and bewilderment of each of us and of our world he will come at last to heal and to save.

When Jesus of Nazareth rode into Jerusalem on Palm Sunday and his followers cried out, "Blessed is the King who comes in the name of the Lord," the Pharisees went to Jesus and told him to put an end to their blasphemies, and Jesus said to them, "I tell you, if these were silent, the very stones would cry out."

This church. The church on the other side of town, the other side of the world. All churches everywhere. The day will come when they will lie in ruins, every last one of them. The day will come when all the voices that were ever raised in them, including our own, will be permanently stilled. But when that day comes, I believe that the tumbled stones will cry aloud of the great, deep hope that down through the centuries has been the one reason for having churches at all and is the one reason we have for coming to this one now: the hope that into the world the King does come. And in the name of the Lord. And is always coming, blessed be he. And will come afire with glory, at the end of time.

In the meantime, King Jesus, we offer all churches to you as you offer them to us. Make thyself known in them. Make thy will done in them. Make our stone hearts cry out thy kingship. Make us holy and human at last that we may do the work of thy love.

4. Love

DEUTERONOMY 6:4–7

Hear, O Israel: the Lord our God is one Lord and you shall love the Lord your God with all your heart, and with all your soul, and with all your might. And these words which I command you this day shall be upon your heart; and you shall teach them diligently to your children, and shall talk of them when you sit in your house, and when you walk by the way, and when you lie down, and when you rise.

MATTHEW 27:45, 46

Now from the sixth hour there was darkness over all the land until the ninth hour. And about the ninth hour Jesus cried with a loud voice, "Eli, Eli, lama sabachthani?" that is "My God, my God, why hast thou forsaken me?"

"Hear, O Israel!" says the great text in Deuteronomy where Moses calls out to his people in the wilderness. Hear, O Israel! *Hear!* Listen! And not just O Israel, hear, but O World, O Everybody, O Thou, O every last man and woman of us because we are all of us called to become Israel by hearing lest instead we become Israel by not hearing and thus like her in her apostasy instead of in her faith. Nor is it just the text in Deuteronomy that is calling out to us to hear but the entire text of the Bible as a whole. We are to hear. All of us are. That is what the whole Bible is calling out. *"Hear, O Israel!"*

But hear what? Hear what? The Bible is hundreds upon hundreds of voices all calling at once out of the past and clamoring for our attention like barkers at a fair, like air-raid sirens, like a whole barnyard of cockcrows as the first long shafts of dawn fan out across the sky. Some of the voices are shouting, like Moses' voice, so all Israel, all the world, can hear, and some are so soft and halting that you can hardly hear them at all, like Job with ashes on his head and his heart broken, like old Simeon whispering, "Lord, now lettest thou thy servant depart in peace." The prophets shrill out in their frustration, their rage, their holy hope and madness; and the priests drone on and on about the dimensions and furniture of the Temple; and the lawgivers spell out what to eat and what not to eat; and the historians list the kings, the battles, the tragic lessons of Israel's history. And somewhere in the midst of them all one particular voice speaks out that is unlike any other voice because it speaks so directly to the deepest privacy and longing and weariness of each of us that there are times when the centuries are blown away like mist, and it is as if we stand with no shelter of time at all between ourselves and the one who speaks our secret name. *Come,* the voice says. *Unto me. All ye.* Every last one.

Hear! the Bible says. Hear, O Israel! And what there is to hear is so vast and varied that it can be like sitting in the thick of a crowd so huge and clamorous that you literally don't know what all the shouting is about. You have to go stand across the street somewhere under the stars. You have to elbow your way out of the great crowd. And maybe then—off by yourself with some distance to catch your breath in and to soften the sound—maybe then you hear, in a sudden burst of cheering or windy gasp of astonishment as it rises up out of the huge arena, the inner truth of what all the shouting is about.

And that, I believe, is what this text from Deuteronomy does. It gives us distance and perspective. It sounds the one crucial and definitive note that points to the heart of the great crowd's thundering. "You shall love the Lord your God with all your heart, and with all your soul, and with all your might." That is what you are to hear. That is the heart of it, Deuteronomy says. And then, century upon century later, the Pharisees come and ask, "Teacher, what is the great commandment?" and the words that Jesus answers them with are the same words. "You shall love the Lord your God with all your heart, and with all your soul, and with all your might. This is the first and great commandment."

Love God. We have heard the words so often that we no longer hear them. They are too loud to hear, too big to take in. We know the words so much *by* heart that we scarcely know them any longer as words spoken *to* the heart out of a mystery beyond all knowing. We take the words so much for granted that we hardly stop to wonder where they are seeking to take us. Above all else, the words say, *you shall love*—not, first your neighbor as yourself because that is second and comes later. On the contrary, it is God you shall love first before you love anything else, and you shall love him with all that you are and all that you have it in you to become—whatever that means, whatever that involves. The words don't explain. They just proclaim and command.

Loving our neighbors, loving each other, is easier to talk about, easier even to do. God knows we are none of us much good at it much of the time, but at least we can see each other with our eyes. We can see each other's faces especially, and every once in a while, if we have our eyes open, we can see something of what is within those faces. Even with strangers sometimes—people we pass on the street or find sitting across from us in a bus or a waiting room; even sometimes with people we know very well but seldom take the trouble really to look at—we see something that stops us in our tracks. We catch a glimpse of some unexpected beauty or pain or need in another's face, or maybe we just notice the tilt of an old man's Agway cap, or the way a young woman rests her cheek on the palm of her hand, or the way a child looks out the window at the rain; and for a moment, then, our heart goes out to them in ways too deep for words. We would love them right if we only could. We would love them truly and forever if we only knew how. And even as things are, we love them maybe as much as we are capable of loving anybody.

But so much of our loving them has to do with seeing them—these strangers who are sometimes so precious, these precious ones who are sometimes such strangers— whereas the God we are commanded to love with all our hearts, souls, might, is the one we cannot see at all. Not even Moses could see him when he asked to because humans shall not see him and live, God said. "I will put you in a cleft of the rock," God said, "and I will cover you with my hand until I have passed by . . . and you shall see my back; but my face shall not be seen" (Exod. 33:22, 23).

We also have seen God's back, or pray at least that that is what we have seen. We have seen traces of him in each other's faces and in the mystery and splendor of the creation maybe; have seen as much of him as human eyes can see in the dream each of us has of Christ's face. But him in himself, God in his full glory and power, we have not seen and cannot see, and yet it is he whom we are commanded to love above all others. *Hear, O Israel!* You shall love him.

Can we? Do we even know what loving God looks like and feels like—not just taking comfort in him as an idea, not just believing in him as a possibility, not just worshiping him (because there was never a man or woman yet who didn't have to worship something, so why not God?), but actually loving him: wanting at least to be near him, wanting at least to do things for him, because that is the least of what love seems to mean?

If we have never seen God, maybe we can say at least that we have heard him. Maybe "hearing" is a better metaphor than "seeing" and certainly a more Biblical one because hearing takes place in time: we listen to one word following another in time, and it is in time, in the day-by-day events of our own times and of historic time, that God makes himself known to us if he makes himself known to us at all. And in this sense of "hearing," we can sometimes believe that we have heard him for ourselves. We have heard him in Scripture—in the passion of Jeremiah, the crying out of Job, the love of Christ. We have heard him in history. We have heard him in our own inner histories —our own passion, our own crying out, our own love.

And yet, to be honest, we must say also that there are times when we have not heard him any more than we have seen him. There are times when we have heard the Bible, the Gospels themselves, ring like a cracked bell. When we have heard truth itself go sour, banal, ambiguous, have listened to our own lives and heard mostly confusion and emptiness. Instead of hearing God, there have been times when we have heard only a Godforsaken silence. And for many of us these are the times that we know best.

Hear, O Israel! Only more often than not we hear nothing because we live in a wilderness where more often than not there is nothing of God to hear. And of course it was in just such a wilderness that the great words of Moses were trumpeted forth in the first place, and the people who first heard them were in the wilderness with him, as wandering and lost as we are, with nothing to keep them going but the hope of a Promised Land which much of the time seemed a promise so remote and improbable that even the bondage they had left behind them in Egypt looked hopeful by comparison. To be commanded to love God at all, let alone in the wilderness, is like being commanded to be well when we are sick, to sing for joy when we are dying of thirst, to run when our legs are broken. But this is the first and great commandment nonetheless. Even in the wilderness—especially in the wilderness—you shall love him.

We know that wilderness well, you and I—all of us do —because there isn't one of us who hasn't wandered there, lost, and who will not wander there again before our time is done. Let me speak for a moment of once when I wandered there myself. The wilderness was a strange city three thousand miles from home. In a hospital in that city there was somebody I loved as much as I have ever loved anybody, and she was in danger of dying. Apparently not even death itself was as terrifying to her as life was, and for that reason she was fighting against her own healing. With part of herself she didn't want to be well. She had lost track of what being well meant, and day after day my wife and I drove to the hospital to see her, parked the car in the parking lot, went up in the elevator. We played games with her. We rubbed her back. We read aloud. She weighed less as a young woman than she had as a child. We had known her since the day she was born, but if we had passed her in the corridor, we wouldn't have been able to recognize her.

When the worst finally happens, or almost happens, a kind of peace comes. I had passed beyond grief, beyond terror, all but beyond hope, and it was there, in that wilderness, that for the first time in my life I caught sight of something of what it must be like to love God truly. It was only a glimpse, but it was like stumbling on fresh water in the desert, like remembering something so huge and extraordinary that my memory had been unable to contain it. Though God was nowhere to be clearly seen, nowhere to be clearly heard, I had to be near him—even in the elevator riding up to her floor, even walking down the corridor to the one door among all those doors that had her name taped on it. I loved him because there was nothing else left. I loved him because he seemed to have made himself as helpless in his might as I was in my helplessness. I loved him not so much in spite of there being nothing in it for me but almost because there was nothing in it for me. For the first time in my life, there in that wilderness, I caught a glimpse of what it must be like to love God truly, for his own sake, to love him no matter what. If I loved him with less than all my heart, soul, might, I loved him with at least as much of them as I had left for loving anything.

And in that wilderness several small things happened that were not of that wilderness because they were of a far country. Two total strangers found their way to me, both of them ministers, offering more than just help because what they offered was themselves in a way that made me understand for the first time what the word *Christendom* means—Christ's domain or dominion, the King's kingdom. And one night I heard compline sung in a great, bare church—sat in the coolness and dimness of it with nothing I had to say or be or do except just to let the chanting voices—grave, dispassionate, unearthly—wash over me like air from a far country. And quite by accident—if there are such things as accidents at times like these—I opened the Bible one evening to the 131st Psalm, which, if I'd ever read it before, I had read only as words but which became now—of all words—the ones I most needed to hear: "O Lord, my heart is not lifted up, my eyes are not raised too high; I do not occupy myself with things too great and too marvelous for me. But I have calmed and quieted my soul, like a child quieted at its mother's breast; like a child that is quieted is my soul. O Israel, hope in the Lord from this time forth and for evermore."

I did not love God, God knows, because I was some sort of saint or hero. I did not love him because I suddenly saw the light (there was almost no light at all) or because I hoped by loving him to persuade him to heal the young woman I loved. I loved him because I couldn't help myself. I loved him because the one who commands us to love is the one who also empowers us to love, as there in the wilderness of that dark and terrible time I was, through no doing of my own, empowered to love him at least a little, at least enough to survive. And in the midst of it, these small things happened that were as big as heaven and earth because through them a hope beyond hopelessness happened. "O Israel, hope in the Lord from this time forth and for evermore."

O Israel, hope. Have faith. Above all, love. You shall

love the Lord your God. That is the first and greatest. And
I suppose the truth of it is something like this: that as the
farthest reach of our love for each other is loving our
enemies, and as the farthest reach of God's love for us is
loving us at our most unlovable and unlovely, so the farthest reach of our love for God is loving him when in
almost every way that matters we can neither see him nor
hear him, and when he himself might as well be our enemy
for all he comes to us in the ways we want him to come,
and when the worst of the wilderness for us is the fear that
he has forsaken us if indeed he exists at all.

"My God, my God, why hast thou forsaken me?" As
Christ speaks those words, he too is in the wilderness. He
speaks them when all is lost. He speaks them when there
is nothing even he can hear except for the croak of his own
voice and when as far as even he can see there is no God
to hear him. And in a way his words are a love song, the
greatest love song of them all. In a way his words are the
words we all of us must speak before we know what it
means to love God as we are commanded to love him.

"My God, *my* God." Though God is not there for him
to see or hear, he calls on him still because he can do no
other. Not even the cross, not even death, not even life,
can destroy his love for God. Not even God can destroy
his love for God because the love he loves God with is
God's love empowering him to love in return with all his
heart even when his heart is all but broken.

That is the love that you and I are called to move
toward both through the wilderness times, on broken legs,
and through times when we catch glimpses and hear whispers from beyond the wilderness. Nobody ever claimed
the journey was going to be an easy one. It is not easy to

love God with all your heart and soul and might when much of the time you have all but forgotten his name. But to love God is not a goal we have to struggle toward on our own because what at its heart the Gospel is all about is that God himself moves us toward it even when we believe he has forsaken us.

The final secret, I think, is this: that the words "You shall love the Lord your God" become in the end less a command than a promise. And the promise is that, yes, on the weary feet of faith and the fragile wings of hope, we will come to love him at last as from the first he has loved us—loved us even in the wilderness, especially in the wilderness, because he has been in the wilderness with us. He has been in the wilderness for us. He has been acquainted with our grief. And, loving him, we will come at last to love each other too so that, in the end, the name taped on every door will be the name of the one we love.

"And these words which I command you this day shall be upon your heart; and you shall teach them diligently to your children, and you shall talk of them when you sit in your house, and when you walk by the way, and when you rise."

And rise we shall, out of the wilderness, every last one of us, even as out of the wilderness Christ rose before us. That is the promise, and the greatest of all promises.

5. The Two Stories

2 CORINTHIANS 2:14–17

But thanks be to God, who in Christ always leads us in triumph, and through us spreads the fragrance of the knowledge of him everywhere. For we are the aroma of Christ to God among those who are being saved and among those who are perishing, to one a fragrance from death to death, to the other a fragrance from life to life. Who is sufficient for these things? For we are not, like so many, peddlers of God's word; but as men of sincerity, as commissioned by God, in the sight of God we speak in Christ.

A few months ago I received a letter inviting me to speak to a group of ministers on the subject of story-telling. It was a good letter and posed a number of thoughtful questions such as: How do you use stories effectively in sermons? How do you use a story to put a point across? To what degree do you make the point of your story clear to your listeners instead of leaving them to work it out for themselves? And so on. They were all perfectly reasonable questions to which I think useful answers can be given, but the more I thought about them and how I might set about trying to answer them, the more I found that something about them gave me pause. The trouble was that they were all questions that had to do with *how* to tell a story instead of *what* stories to tell and *to what end;* and the kind of stories they rightly or wrongly suggested to me were stories as anecdotes, as attention-getters, as illustrations, stories to hang on sermons like lights on a Christmas tree. Maybe I did the letter-writer an injustice, and that isn't what he had in mind at all, but if so, all I can say is that that's the kind of stories I have often heard in church myself. And why not? They have their place. They can help make the medicine go down. But the more I thought about it, the more I realized that even if I believed I could give some helpful literary advice along those lines, that was not what basically interested me.

And yet what the letter reminded me of is that yes, story-telling is itself immensely interesting and immensely important. Not just for preachers and preachers-to-be but for Christians in general. Story-telling matters enormously because it is a story, of course, which stands at the heart of our faith and which more perhaps than any other form of discourse speaks to our hearts and illumines our own stories. It is related to what Paul is writing about, I think, in this passage from Corinthians. "We are not, like so many, peddlers of God's word," he says, and the image is a rich and painfully telling one.

Peddlers are people with packs on their backs full of things they want to sell, and the things they try to sell hardest are the things they think will sell best. Peddlers are less concerned with what the world needs than with what the world wants or can be made to settle for. Peddlers are salespeople who are interested less in the quality of what they're selling than in the success of their sale. So if the peddlers of God's word happen to be preachers, it's preaching as an end in itself that they're apt to concentrate on. They do their best to be effective, eloquent, original.

They choose the stories that will go over best and be remembered to their credit longest. Or if we happen not to be preachers, then when it comes to just speaking of, and out of, our faith in a general way, we, like them, tend to stick to the salesmanship of it and to speak of it whatever is easiest to speak and whatever we think will go down most easily.

We speak of books we've read and ideas we've had. We speak of great questions like abortion and conservation and the dangers of nuclear power, and of what we take to be the Christian answers to such questions. If we get more personal about it, we speak of problems we've had—problems with children and old age, problems with sex and marriage, ethical problems—and of Christian solutions to those problems or at least of Christian ways of viewing them. And if, in the process, we decide to tell stories, then, like the preacher as peddler, we may tell stories about ourselves as well as about other people but not, for the most part, our real stories, not stories about what lies beneath all our other problems, which is the problem of being human, the problem of trying to hold fast somehow to Christ when much of the time, both in ourselves and in our world, it is as if Christ had never existed. Because all peddlers of God's word have that in common, I think: they tell what costs them least to tell and what will gain them most; and to tell the story of who we really are, and of the battle between light and dark, between belief and unbelief, between sin and grace that is waged within us all, costs plenty and may not gain us anything, we're afraid, but an uneasy silence and a fishy stare.

So one way or another we are all of us peddlers of

God's word, and those of us in the ministry are more apt to be peddlers than most because, as professionals, we're continually being sought out to display our wares. We're invited to give commencement addresses and to speak about story-telling to people who travel miles to learn the trick. And so it's to all of us that Paul speaks. "We are not," he says (meaning we should not be, must not be, had bloody well better not be), "we are not, like so many, peddlers of God's word; but as men of sincerity, commissioned by God, in the sight of God we speak in Christ." That's the whole point of it, he says: *to speak in Christ,* which means among other things, I assume, to speak *of* Christ. And when it comes to story-telling, that is of course the crux of it. If we are to speak, as he says, with sincerity —speak as we have been commissioned by God to speak, and with our hearts as well as our lips—then this is the one story above all others that we have in us to tell, you and I. It is his story.

The story of Christ is where we all started from, though we've come so far since then that there are times when you'd hardly know it to listen to us and when we hardly know it ourselves. The story of Christ is what once, somehow and somewhere, we came to Christ through. Maybe it happened little by little—a face coming slowly into focus that we'd been looking at for a long time without really seeing it, a voice gradually making itself heard among many other voices and in such a way that we couldn't help listening after a while, couldn't help trying somehow, in some unsatisfactory way, to answer. Or maybe there was more drama to it than that—a sudden catch of the breath at the sound of his name on somebody's lips at a moment we weren't expecting it, a sudden welling up of tears out of a place where we didn't think any tears were. Each of us has a tale to tell if we would only tell it. But however it happened, it comes to seem a long time ago and a long way away, and so many things have happened since—so many books read, so many sermons heard or preached, so much life lived—that to be reminded at this stage of the game of the story of Jesus, where we all started, is like being suddenly called by your childhood name when you have all but forgotten your childhood name and maybe your childhood too.

The Jehovah's Witness appears on the doorstep, or somebody who's gotten religion corners you at a party, and embarrassing questions are asked in an embarrassing language. Have you been born again? Have you accepted Jesus Christ as your personal Lord and savior? And yes, yes, you want to say—half humiliated, half appalled and irritated, torn in a dozen directions at once by the directness and corn of it, tongue-tied. You wouldn't be caught dead maybe using such language yourself, but oh Jesus, yes, in some sense your answer is and has to be yes, though to be asked it out of the blue that way, by a stranger you'd never have opened the door to if you'd known what he was after, makes the blood run cold. To be reminded that way or any way of the story of Jesus, where you came from, is like having somebody suddenly produce a picture of home in all its homeliness—the barn that needs cleaning, the sagging porch steps, the face in the dusty window —when you've traveled a thousand miles and a thousand years from home and are involved in a thousand new and different things. But the story of Jesus is home nonetheless —the barn, the steps, the face. You belong to it. It belongs to you. It is where you came from. God grant it is also where you are heading for. So that is the story to remember. That is the story beyond all stories to tell.

The story of Jesus is full of darkness as well as of light. It is a story that hides more than it reveals. It is the story of a mystery we must never assume we understand and that comes to us breathless and broken with unspeakable beauty at the heart of it yet by no means a pretty story though that is the way we're apt to peddle it much of the time. We sand down the rough edges. We play down the obscurities and contradictions. What we can't explain, we explain away. We set Jesus forth as clear-eyed and noble-browed whereas the chances are he can't have been anything but old before his time once the world started working him over and, once the world was through, his clear eyes swollen shut and his noble brow as much of a shambles as the rest of him. We're apt to tell his story when we tell it at all, to sell his story, for the poetry and panacea of it. "But we are the aroma of Christ," Paul says, and the story we are given to tell is a story that smells of his life in all its aliveness, and our commission is to tell it in a way that makes it come alive as a story in all its aliveness and to make those who hear it come alive and God knows to make ourselves come alive too.

He was born, the story begins—the barn that needs cleaning, the sagging steps, the dusty face—and there are times when we have to forget all about the angels and shepherds and star of it, I think, and just let the birth as a birth be wonder enough, which Heaven help us it is, this wonder of all wonders. Into a world that has never been famous for taking special care of the naked and helpless, he was born in the same old way to the same old end and in all likelihood howled bloody murder with the rest of us when they got the breath going in him and he sensed more or less what he was in for. An old man in the Temple predicted great things for him but terrible things for the mother who loved him in what seem to have been all the wrong ways. He got lost in the city and worried his parents sick. John baptized him in the river and wondered afterwards if he'd chosen the right man. It wasn't just Satan who tempted him then because for the rest of his life just about everybody tempted him—his best friend, his disciples, his mother and brothers, his enemies. They all of them tempted him one way or another not to go off the deep end but to stay on the bearable surface of things— to work miracles you could see with your eyes, to feed hungers you could feel in your belly, to heal the sickness of the flesh you could touch, to be a power among powers and to avoid the powerless, the sinful, the deadbeats like the plague in favor of the outwardly righteous, the publicly pious.

But "like a root out of dry ground," he came, Isaiah says, and it was down at the roots of things that he moved all his life like a mole—down at the undetected sickness fiercer than flesh, the buried sin, the hidden holiness. "Cleave the wood, I am there," he says in the apocryphal Gospel of Thomas. "Lift the stone, and you will find me there," and it is always far beneath that he is to be found and deep within that his most shattering miracles happen. He made precious few friends and a mob of enemies. He taught in a way that almost nobody either understood or wanted to risk understanding, least of all the ones who were closest to him. And in the end they got him. And forget all the grim paraphernalia of his death because the obscenity and horror have long since been ritualized out of it. They got him, that's all. He wasn't spared a damned thing. It was awful beyond telling, god-awful. And then it happened.

However we try to explain it, however we try at all costs to avoid having to explain it because it was so long ago and seems so wild and crazy and because so many other more plausible, manageable things have happened since; whatever words we can find for telling the story or for watering it down—what happened was that he wasn't dead anymore. He wasn't dead. Anymore. He was not a ghost. By comparison, it's we who are the ghosts. The worst we know of darkness, any of us, was split in two like an atom. The explosion shook history to its roots, shook even us once to our roots though it's sometimes hard to remember. The fall-out continues to this day—falls imperceptibly, without a sound, like snow or ash, like light. Only it is not death-dealing. It is life-dealing. You and I are here in this place now because of what little life it dealt us. Because of this story of Jesus, each of our own stories is in countless ways different from what it would have been otherwise, and that is why in speaking about him we must speak also about ourselves and about ourselves with him and without him too because that, of course, is the other story we have in us to remember and tell. Our own story.

We are men and women of sincerity, Paul says, and God help us if we're not because that's what we're cracked up to be, and sincerity you'd like to think would be the least of it. We are commissioned by God to speak in Christ, and to speak in Christ is to speak truth, and there is no story whose truth we are closer to than our own, than the story of what it's like to live inside ourselves. The trouble is that, like Christ's story, this too is apt to be the last we tell, partly because we are uncomfortable with it and afraid of sincerity and partly because we have half forgotten it. But tell it we must and, before we tell it to anybody else, tell it first of all to ourselves and keep on telling it because unless we do, unless we live with, and out of, the story of who we are inside ourselves, we lose track of who we are. We live so much on the outer surface and seeming of our lives and our faith that we lose touch with the deep places that they both come from.

We have the story of our own baptism, for one—if not by water, in a river, then by fire God knows where, because there isn't one of us whose life hasn't flamed up into moments when a door opened somewhere that let the future in, moments when we moved through that door as Jesus moved out of Jordan, not perfectly cleansed but cleansed enough, with the past behind us, we hoped, and a new sense of what at its most outlandish and holiest the future might become. And God knows we have all had our wilderness and our temptations too—not the temptation to work evil probably, because by grace or luck we don't have what it takes for more than momentary longings in that direction, but the temptation to settle for the lesser good, which is evil enough and maybe a worse one—to settle for niceness and usefulness and busyness instead of for holiness; to settle for plausibility and eloquence instead of for truth. And miracles too are part of our story as well as of his, blind though we are to them most of the time and leery as we are of acknowledging them because to acknowledge a miracle is to have to act on it somehow—to become some kind of miracles ourselves—and that's why they scare us to death. But the miracle of our own births when the odds were millions to one against them. The miracle of every right turn we ever took and every healing word we ever spoke. The miracle of loving sometimes even the unlovely, and out of our own unloveliness. And the half-forgotten miracles by which we've turned up here now, such as we are, who might never have made it here at all when you consider all the hazards along the way.

And crucifixion is part of our stories too, because we too are men and women of sorrow and acquainted with grief. Maybe our crucifixion is in knowing that for all we'd like to believe to the contrary, we don't have the stomach for even such few, half-baked chances to give up something precious for him as come our way, let alone for giving up, in any sense that really matters, our selves for him. Yet we're raised up nonetheless. We're raised up, and we have that to tell of too, that part of our story. In spite of every reason to give the whole show up, we're here still just able to hope; in spite of all the griefs and failures we've known, we're here still just able to rejoice; in spite of the darkness that we all of us flirt with, we are here still just a little, at least, in love with light. By miracle we survive even our own shabbiness, and for the time being maybe that is resurrection enough.

Two stories then—our own story and Jesus' story, and in the end, perhaps, they are the same story. "Cleave the wood, I am there. Lift up the stone, and you will find me there." To cleave the truth of our own lives, to lift and look beneath our own stories, is to see glimmers at least of his life, of his life struggling to come alive in our lives, his story whispering like a song through the babble and drone of ours. Where he is strong, we are weak, God knows. Where he is faithful, we are what we are. Where he opens himself to the worst the world can do, for the sake of the best the world can be, we arm ourselves against the world with the world's hard armor for our own sweet sakes. Our stories are at best a parody of his story, and if, as Paul says, we are the fragrance of Christ, then it is like the fragrance of the sea from ten miles inland when the wind is in the right direction, like the fragrance of a rose from the other side of the street, with all the world between.

Yet they meet as well as diverge, our stories and his, and even when they diverge, it is *his* they diverge from, so that by his absence as well as by his presence in our lives we know who he is and who we are and who we are not.

We have it in us to be Christs to each other and maybe in some unimaginable way to God too—that's what we have to tell finally. We have it in us to work miracles of love and healing as well as to have them worked upon us. We have it in us to bless with him and forgive with him and heal with him and once in a while maybe even to grieve with some measure of his grief at another's pain and to rejoice with some measure of his rejoicing at another's joy almost as if it were our own. And who knows but that in the end, by God's mercy, the two stories will converge for good and all, and though we would never have had the courage or the faith or the wit to die for him any more than we have ever managed to live for him very well either, his story will come true in us at last. And in the meantime, this side of Paradise, it is our business (not, like so many, peddlers of God's word but as men and women of sincerity) to speak with our hearts (which is what sincerity means) and to bear witness to, and live out of, and live toward, and live by, the true word of his holy story as it seeks to stammer itself forth through the holy stories of us all.

6. Emmanuel

MATTHEW 1:23
"Behold, a virgin shall conceive and bear a son, and his name
shall be called Emmanuel" (which means, God with us).

"For we preach Christ crucified," the Apostle Paul wrote
to the church at Corinth, "a stumbling block to Jews and
folly to Gentiles." He could as well have written "We
preach Christ born" or "We preach Christmas" because
the birth presents no fewer problems than the death does
both to religious people—"the Jews"—and to everybody
else—"the Gentiles." Christmas is not just Mr. Pickwick
dancing a reel with the old lady at Dingley Dell or
Scrooge waking up the next morning a changed man. It
is not just the spirit of giving abroad in the land with a
white beard and reindeer. It is not just the most famous
birthday of them all and not just the annual reaffirmation
of Peace on Earth that it is often reduced to so that people
of many faiths or no faith can exchange Christmas cards
without a qualm. On the contrary, if you do not hear in
the message of Christmas something that must strike some
as blasphemy and others as sheer fantasy, the chances are
you have not heard the message for what it is. *Emmanuel*
is the message in a nutshell, which is Hebrew for "God

with us." Who is this God? How is he with us? That's where the problem lies.

God is "the high and lofty One who inhabits eternity," says the prophet Isaiah, and by and large, though they would use different language and symbols to express it, all the major faiths of the world would tend to agree. Judaism calls him Yahweh. Islam calls him Allah. Buddhism and Hinduism use terms like Brahman-Atman or the Void or the One. But whatever they call him, all of them point to the ultimate spiritual Ground of existence as transcendent and totally other. The reality of God is so radically different from anything we know as real that in the last analysis we can say nothing about him except what he is not. *Neti neti* is the Upanishad's famous definition: he is not this, he is not that. "The Tao that can be expressed is not the eternal Tao" says the *Tao Te Ching* of Taoism. The Old Testament says it in characteristically concrete form as a narrative. When Moses asks to see God, God answers by saying, "You cannot see my face, for man cannot see me and live." As a mark of special favor, he hides Moses in the cleft of a rock and only after he has passed by in his glory takes his hand away so that Moses can see his back. According to the Protestant theologian Paul Tillich, you cannot even say that God exists in the same sense that you say a person exists, or a mountain or an idea. God is not a thing among other things. He does not take his place in a prior reality. He is that out of which reality itself arises, and to say that "he is" as we say that "we are" is to use language that is at best crudely metaphoric.

If all this sounds hopelessly abstruse, it nonetheless reflects the common experience of human beings as they contemplate the mystery that surrounds them. When a person looks up at the stars and ponders that which either goes on forever or ends at some unthinkably remote point beyond which there is Nothing; when we pray out of our deepest need to a God whom we can know only through faith; when we confront the enigma of our own life and the inevitability of our own death, all we can do is hold our tongues or say with Job, "Behold, I am of small account. I lay my hand on my mouth. . . . I have uttered what I did not understand, things too wonderful for me, which I did not know."

That is not the end of it, of course. Transcendent as God is—of another quality entirely from the world that he transcends—he nonetheless makes himself known to the world. Many would say that he is known to it because he made it, and from their earliest beginnings, people have looked at the world of nature and claimed to see in it the marks of his handicraft. Where nature is beautiful and beneficent, they have seen the love of God and where it is harsh and terrifying, his wrath. In the orderliness of nature they have seen God as lawgiver, and where this order is interrupted by the unforeseen and chaotic, they have seen miracle. And the same holds true for the world of history. The prosperity of nations or individuals suggests God's favor, and disaster suggests either condemnation or warning. Even the religions of India, which see the world less as the creation of the Ultimate than as a kind of illusory reverberation of it, speak of the law of karma which as inexorably as the law of gravity rewards the good and punishes the evil. Furthermore, though they do not see the world as a book where humankind can read of the nature and will of God but rather as an endless cycle of death and rebirth where our only hope is to escape altogether into the ineffable bliss of Nirvana, the very fact that such escape is available suggests the presence of something not entirely unlike divine intervention. Indeed, great teaching Buddhas and infinitely compassionate Bodhisattvas keep reappearing throughout the ages to show the way to Nirvana just as in the Biblically based religions of Judaism, Islam, and Christianity, God keeps sending forth prophets, saints, angels.

And in all these traditions, needless to say, God also makes himself known through the mystics. However religions differ in other ways, all of them produce men and women who, by turning their attention inward, encounter him at first hand. As different from one another as Teresa of Avila, Ramakrishna, Thomas Merton, and using language that varies from the Bhagavad Gita to the journals of the Quaker George Fox, they all clearly seem to be trying to express the same ecstatic and inexpressible experience which might best be summarized as, at one and the same time, the total loss and total realization of self in merging with the ultimately Real.

Back then to the essential message of Christmas which is Emmanuel, God with us, and to the questions it raises: Who is this God and how is he with us? "The high and lofty One who inhabits eternity" is the answer to the first. The One who is with us is the One whom none can look upon because the space-and-time human mind can no more comprehend fully the spaceless, timeless Reality of the One than the eyes of the blind can comprehend light. The One who is with us is the One who has made himself known at most only partially and dimly through the pantomime of nature and history and the eloquent but always garbled utterance of prophets, saints, and mystics.

It is the answer to the second question that seems "folly to the Gentiles" and "a stumbling block to the Jews" because the claim that Christianity makes for Christmas is that at a particular time and place God came to be with us himself. When Quirinius was governor of Syria, in a town called Bethlehem, a child was born who, beyond the power of anyone to account for, was the high and lofty One made low and helpless. The One who inhabits eternity comes to dwell in time. The One whom none can look upon and live is delivered in a stable under the soft, indifferent gaze of cattle. The Father of all mercies puts himself at our mercy.

For those who believe in the transcendence and total otherness of God, it radically diminishes him. For those who do not believe in God, it is the ultimate absurdity. For those who stand somewhere between belief and unbelief, it challenges credulity in a new way. It is not a theory that can be tested rationally because it is beyond reason and because it is not a theory, not something that theologians have thought their way to. The claim is, instead, that it is something that has happened, and reason itself is somehow tested by it, humankind's whole view of what is possible and real. Year after year the ancient tale of what happened is told—raw, preposterous, holy—and year after year the world in some measure stops to listen.

In the winter of 1947 a great snow fell on New York City. It began slowly, undramatically, like any other snow. The flakes were fine and steady and fell straight, with no wind. Little by little the sidewalks started to whiten. Shopkeepers and doormen were out with their shovels clearing paths to the street. After a while the streets began to fill and the roofs of parked cars were covered. You could no

longer tell where the curb was, and even the hydrants
disappeared, the melted discs over manhole covers. The
plows could not keep up with it, and traffic moved more
and more slowly as the drifts piled up. Businesses closed
early, and people walked home from work. All evening it
continued falling and much of the night. There were skiers
on Park Avenue, children up way past their bedtime. By
the next morning it was a different city. More striking than
anything else about it was the silence. All traffic had
stopped. Abandoned cars were buried. Nothing on
wheels moved. The only sounds to be heard were church
bells and voices. You listened because you could not help
yourself.

"Ice splits starwise," Sir Thomas Browne wrote. A tap
of the pick at the right point, and fissures shoot out in all
directions, and the solid block falls in two at the star. The
child is born, and history itself falls in two at the star.
Whether you believe or do not believe, you date your
letters and checks and income tax forms with a number
representing how many years have gone by since what
happened happened. The world of A.D. is one world, and
the world of B.C. is another. Whatever the mystery was
that widened the gaze of Tutankhamen's golden head, it
was not this mystery. Whatever secret triggered the ar-
chaic smiles of Argive marbles or made the Bodhisattvas
sit bolt upright at Angkor Vat, it was not our secret. The
very voices and bells of our world ring out on a different
air, and if most of the time we do not listen, at Christmas
it is hard not to.

Business goes on as usual only moreso. Canned carols
blast out over shopping center blacktops before the
Thanksgiving turkey is cold on the plate. Salvation Army

tambourines rattle, and streetcorner Santas stamp their feet against the cold. But if you have an ear for it at all, at the heart of all the hullabaloo you hear a silence, and at the heart of the silence you hear—whatever you hear.

"The Word became flesh and dwelt among us, full of grace and truth," the prologue to the Gospel of John says. A dream as old as time of the God descending hesitates on the threshold of coming true in a way to make all other truths seem dreamlike. If it is true, it is the chief of all truths. If it is not true, it is of all truths the one perhaps that people would most have be true if they could make it so. Maybe it is that longing to have it be true that is at the bottom even of the whole vast Christmas industry— the tons of cards and presents and fancy food, the plastic figures kneeling on the floodlit lawns of poorly attended churches. The world speaks of holy things in the only language it knows, which is a worldly language.

Emmanuel. We all must decide for ourselves whether it is true. Certainly the grounds on which to dismiss it are not hard to find. Christmas is commercialism. It is a pain in the neck. It is sentimentality. It is wishful thinking. With its account of the shepherds, the star, the three wise men, it smacks of a make-believe pathetically out of place in a world of energy crisis and space exploration and economic *malaise.* Yet it is never as easy to get rid of as all this makes it sound because whereas to dismiss belief in God is to dismiss only an idea, an hypothesis, for which there are many alternatives (such as belief in no god at all or in any of the lesser gods we are always creating for ourselves like Science or Morality or the inevitability of human progress), to dismiss Christmas is for most of us to dismiss part of ourselves.

For one thing it is to dismiss one of the most fragile yet enduring visions of our own childhood and of the child that continues to exist in all of us. The sense of mystery and wonderment. The sense that on this one day each year two plus two adds up not to four but to a million. The leap of the heart at waking up into a winter morning which for a while at least is as different from all other mornings as the city where the great snow fell was a different city. "Let all mortal flesh keep silence," the old hymn goes, and there was a time for most of us when it did.

And it is to dismiss a face. Who knows what we would have seen if we had been present there in Quirinius's time. Whether it happened the way Luke says it did, with the angels and the star, is almost beside the point because the one thing that believer and unbeliever alike can be equally sure happened is an event that changed the course of human history. And it was a profoundly human event—the birth of a human being by whose humanness we measure our own, of a human being with a face which, though none of us has ever seen it, we would all likely recognize because for twenty centuries it has been of all faces the one that our world has been most haunted by.

More than anything else perhaps, to dismiss this particular birth as no different in kind from the birth of Socrates, say, or Moses or Gautama Buddha would be to dismiss the quality of life that it has given birth to in an astonishing variety of people over an astonishing period of time. There have been wise ones and simple ones, sophisticated ones and crude ones, respectable ones and disreputable ones. There have been medieval peasants and eighteenth-century aristocrats, nineteenth-century spinsters and twentieth-century dropouts. They need not be mystics or saints or even unusually religious in any formal, institutional sense, and there may never have been any one dramatic moment of conversion that they would point to in the past. But somewhere along the line something deep in them split starwise and they became not simply followers of Christ but bearers of his life. A birth of grace and truth took place within them scarcely less miraculous in its way than the one the Magi traveled all those miles to kneel before.

To look at the last great self-portraits of Rembrandt or to read Pascal or hear Bach's B-minor Mass is to know beyond the need for further evidence that if God is anywhere, he is with them, as he is also with the man behind the meat counter, the woman who scrubs floors at Roosevelt Memorial, the high-school math teacher who explains fractions to the bewildered child. And the step from "God with them" to Emmanuel, "God with us," may not be as great as it seems. What keeps the wild hope of Christmas alive year after year in a world notorious for dashing all hopes is the haunting dream that the child who was born that day may yet be born again even in us and our own snowbound, snowblind longing for him.

7. The First Miracle

JOHN 2:1–11

On the third day there was a marriage at Cana in Galilee, and the mother of Jesus was there; Jesus also was invited to the marriage, with his disciples. When the wine failed, the mother of Jesus said to him, "They have no wine." And Jesus said to her, "O woman, what have you to do with me? My hour has not yet come." His mother said to the servants, "Do whatever he tells you." Now six stone jars were standing there, for the Jewish rites of purification, each holding twenty or thirty gallons. Jesus said to them, "Fill the jars with water." And they filled them up to the brim. He said to them, "Now draw some out, and take it to the steward of the feast." So they took it. When the steward of the feast tasted the water now become wine, and did not know where it came from (though the servants who had drawn the water knew), the steward of the feast called the bridegroom and said to him, "Every man serves the good wine first; and when men have drunk freely, then the poor wine; but you have kept the good wine until now." This, the first of his signs, Jesus did at Cana in Galilee, and manifested his glory; and his disciples believed in him.

". . . which holy estate Christ adorned and beautified by his presence and first miracle that he wrought in Cana of Galilee . . ." These are among the opening words of the marriage service in the old *Book of Common Prayer,* and it is well to remind ourselves of the story in the second chapter of John's Gospel that they refer to. There was a wedding feast once in the town of Cana, the story goes, and like all wedding feasts in all towns, it was a great occasion. The bride's family was there, and the bridegroom's family was there—the poor relations and the rich relations, the eccentric aunts and the harried uncles, and as many cousins and friends and assorted well-wishers as the traffic would bear, with the oldest ones resting their bones in the caterer's folding chairs on the sidelines and the youngest ones skittering around underfoot and driving everybody more or less mad. And because it seems that Cana was only a few miles away from the town of Nazareth, Mary was there—Joseph the carpenter's wife—and Jesus of Nazareth was there too, standing around with the rest of them in the midst of all the eating and drinking and general carrying-on with his glass held at shoulder level to keep it from being jostled out of his hand and straining to catch what his mother was trying to say to him above all the racket. He "adorned and beautified it by his presence," the prayer book says—did it just by being there, presumably, just by being who he was, the way anybody we love very much and who loves us very much can more or less do it too.

Then what his mother finally managed to get across to him through all the hubbub was that a crisis had suddenly occurred. Somebody had miscalculated. The wine had run out. Disaster was imminent. Jesus was quite short with her at first when she told him. If it was a miracle she was after, he said, she'd better look elsewhere. He wasn't ready for miracles yet, he said, not ready to be recognized for who he was, not ready for what he knew would be in store for him as soon as he was recognized because he understood as well as you and I do that the world seldom deals very gently with its saints. But then he relented. Who knows why? Maybe just because it was such a good party that he couldn't bear to see it ruined. So he had them fill six stone jars with water and had them take a cupful to the steward of the feast. And as soon as the steward tasted it, his whole face lit up because of course it wasn't water anymore. It was wine and, what's more, not just a common, garden-variety wine either. With his eyes as big as saucers and his beard atremble, the steward said, "Why, usually people serve the best wine first and save the cheap wine for later when nobody's up to telling the difference anymore any-way. But you have saved the best till last!" This was the first sign given by Jesus, the Gospel tells us. It was given in Cana of Galilee. He let his glory be seen.

It's like a fairy tale, of course—full of shadow and mystery and glimmering light. It's like a dream. Did things really happen this way? Was the water really turned into wine, or did it just taste that way because Jesus was there, and when Jesus was there even the ordinary was apt to turn extraordinary—the heart gladdened, the tongue loos-ened, the blood warmed as if by wine? Who can say for sure? We're so good at doubting, so bad at believing, all of us are. But whatever we believe or don't believe about the water changing into wine, there can be no doubt that a miracle took place at that wedding in Cana just as, in a way, a miracle trembles on the threshold of taking place at every wedding.

By all the laws both of logic and simple arithmetic, to give yourself away in love to another would seem to mean that you end up with less of yourself left than you had to begin with. But the miracle is that just the reverse is true, logic and arithmetic go hang. To give yourself away in love to somebody else—as a man and a woman give them-

selves away to each other at a wedding—is to become for
the first time yourself fully. To live not just for yourself
alone anymore but for another self to whom you swear to
be true—plight your troth to, your truth to—is in a new
way to come fully alive. Things needn't have been that
way as far as we know, but that is the way things are, that
is the way life is, and if you and I are inclined to have any
doubts about it, we can always put it to the test. The test,
needless to say, is our lives themselves.

Nobody with any sense claims that marriage is going
to be clear sailing all the way, least of all the author of the
marriage service. "For better for worse, for richer for
poorer, in sickness and in health"—there will be good
times and bad times both. There will be times when the
vows exchanged here—wild and implausible as in countless ways they are—seem all but impossible to keep. But
by holding fast to each other in trust, in patience, in hope,
and by holding fast also to him who has promised to be
present whenever two or three are gathered together in
his name as he was present that day in Cana of Galilee, the
impossible becomes possible. The water becomes wine.
And by grace we become, little by little, human in spite
of ourselves, become whole, become truly loving and
lovely at last.

That is the miracle. And that is why marriage is called
"a holy estate." And that is why Christ "adorned and
beautified it with his presence." And, finally, that is the
sense also in which he "manifested his glory," as the Gospel says, because the glory of Christ is in the long run the
power of Christ to adorn and beautify, to transform and
hallow, the human heart. Our prayer is that he work that—
most precious of all miracles in us all.

8. The Things That Make for Peace

ISAIAH 2:3b, 4

For out of Zion shall go forth the law, and the word of the Lord from Jerusalem. He shall judge between the nations, and shall decide for many peoples; and they shall beat their swords into plowshares, and their spears into pruning hooks; nation shall not lift up sword against nation, neither shall they learn war any more.

LUKE 19:35–44

. . . And throwing their garments on the colt they set Jesus upon it. And as he rode along, they spread their garments on the road. As he was now drawing near, at the descent of the Mount of Olives, the whole multitude of the disciples began to rejoice and praise God with a loud voice for all the mighty works that they had seen, saying, "Blessed is the King who comes in the name of the Lord! Peace in heaven and glory in the highest!" And some of the Pharisees in the multitude said to him, "Teacher, rebuke your disciples." He answered, "I tell you, if these were silent, the very stones would cry out." And when he drew near and saw the city he wept over it, saying, "Would that even today you knew the things that make for peace! But now they are hid from your eyes. For the days shall come upon you, when your enemies will cast up a bank about you and surround you, and hem you in on every side, and dash you to the ground, you and your children within you, and they will not leave one stone upon another in you; because you did not know the time of your visitation."

We call it Palm Sunday because maybe they were palm branches that were thrown into the road in front of him as he approached the city—a kind of poor man's red-carpet treatment, a kind of homemade ticker-tape parade. Just branches is all the record states, but maybe palms is what they actually were, and in any case it's as palms that we remember them; and all over Christendom people leave church with palm leaves of their own to remember him by on the anniversary of his last journey, to pin up on the kitchen bulletin board or stick into the frame of the dresser mirror until finally they turn yellow and brittle with age and we throw them out. Some of the people who were there were so carried away by what was happening that they took the clothes off their backs and spread them out on the road in front of him along with the branches, so that the clip-clop, clip-clop of the hooves of the colt he was riding was muffled by shirts, shawls, cloaks spread out there in the dust as maybe even you and I would have spread ours out too if we'd been there because it was a moment with such hope and passion in it. That's what the palms are all about.

"Blessed is the King who comes in the name of the Lord!" some of them cried out, which are words so rich with mystery that I suspect even the ones who cried them can't have understood them all that much better than you and I do. Blessed? It is hard to understand a blessing so strange and fearsome. At what unimaginable cost blessed? Blessed to what unforeseeable end and with what unforeseeable consequences? And if he was a king, then surely he was like no other king who has ever kinged it on this earth as he trotted along on his bandy-legged little beast with a few old coats thrown over its back for a saddle. But "blessed" they cried out anyway. And "the King" because it was in the name of the Lord that he came, the Lord's anointed King and Messiah whom they saw as the Hope of Israel, the Hope of the World.

Then when some of the opposition who were there by the side of the road too, the Pharisees, heard this shout go up, they were so appalled by the blasphemy of it—this ragged man the Messiah!—that they ran out into the road and told him he'd better shut his friends up before it was too late; and "I tell you," Jesus said, "if these were silent, the very stones would cry out." They are kingly words, and he spoke them like a king. What was starting to kindle in the air of the world as that small procession-of-one wound its way toward the great city was so overwhelming that if no human tongue had told it, he said, the tongue-tied earth itself would have found a tongue to tell it, as I sometimes suspect it tells it even now if we had ears to hear: "Blessed, blessed," as the rain hisses on the face of the sea, "the King, the King" as pebbles knock and rattle against each other with the tide rushing in over them.

We remember this day for what there was of triumph and hope in it, this entry of Jesus into Jerusalem at the start of his last week. Watching him ride into the city again as we've watched him ride into it countless times before is like seeing a famous tragedy acted out on the stage for the hundredth time and yet hoping against hope that maybe this time the impossible will happen and things will somehow go right in the end instead of going wrong—that Juliet will wake up from her drugged sleep before her young lover kills himself, that Cordelia will come alive in the old king's arms so his heart won't have to break after all.

We watch him enter the city hoping against hope that

this time maybe everybody will recognize him for who he is—not just the handful of followers with their palms but the Pharisees too, the Sanhedrin, the High Priest himself. Maybe this time when he is brought before Pilate with his eyes swollen shut and a broken nose, Pilate will sink to his knees before him, and all through the city Romans and Jews, rich men and beggars, saints and thieves, old and young will embrace one another and weep. You can hardly watch him approaching Jerusalem with the sun in his eyes and his bare feet latched under the colt's belly, I think, without almost believing that maybe this time what everybody knows is going to happen will somehow not have to happen and something else will happen instead. Judas will be loyal; Peter will be brave. The cross won't have to happen; and all history will be redeemed without agony; and you and I will go to church or wherever else we go not as strangers—afraid of each other, indifferent to each other, broken and lonely for each other and for God in countless hidden ways—and we won't need any choir to sing for us or preachers to preach for us because just being together under God will be song enough, and no Gospel proclaimed from the pulpit will be as eloquent as the Gospel we live out with each other, and nobody will be a stranger because each of us will be known and cherished by all the rest of us, and there won't be a single face among all the faces we see that won't gladden our hearts like the face of our oldest friend.

Something like that is our hope, I think,—our hope of what might have been, of what still may someday be—and I suspect some hope like that was where the sense of triumph came from that day and was what made them spread their palms and their clothes in the dust and hail

him as they did. But if Jesus himself shared that hope, then
it was a hope blurred and shadowed with sadness because
sadness as well as triumph was in the air like the dust, as
Luke describes it. You picture other parades you have
seen with the heroes of the day raising their arms above
their heads to acknowledge the cheers, nodding and smiling. There is none of that here. You don't picture Jesus
nodding or smiling or raising his arms. On the contrary.
He is silent except when he speaks to the Pharisees. Then
as he draws nearer, Luke says, suddenly he sees the great
city, sees Jerusalem. He comes around a bend in the road
or reaches the top of a hill, and all at once there it is—
ancient and holy even then, built on the high hills with its
walls and domes and parapets shimmering in the spring
sun. Jesus looks at it and weeps, Luke says. "Would that
even today you knew the things that make for peace! But
they are hid from your eyes," he says. "For the days shall
come upon you, when your enemies will . . . dash you to
the ground, you and your children within you, and they
will not leave one stone upon another in you; because you
did not know the time of your visitation."

I wonder if there is any scene in the Gospels that is
more moving, more haunting than that. I wonder if any
sermon preached on those words can add anything to their
eloquence or if there can be any doubts as to what those
words mean. He looked at the city and wept. He does not
weep often in the Gospels, but he weeps here. The palm
branches. The hosannas. The wild shouts of expectancy
and joy. Triumph and hope and healing were what the
shouting was all about that day, and if Palm Sunday ser-
vices are any more than ecclesiastical jamborees, liturgical
vaudeville, then it's because some echo of that shouting is

with us still, some trace of that joy and expectancy glimmers still in our staleness. But if these things were in Jesus' heart too, they were at least not what was uppermost in his heart because when suddenly, around the bend, he saw Jerusalem rising there above him in the hills and he wept, he wept because he knew that in all its beauty—standing there so strong and proud and full of life—the city was doomed. And some forty years later he was proved right, of course. For reasons long since all but forgotten, Jew fought with Roman and Roman with Jew, army warred with army and nation with nation, until finally the walls of Jerusalem, the towers, the Temple, the palaces of priests and kings, the hovels of the poor, all of it was torn down with terrible violence and the city was destroyed as completely as a few centuries later Rome as the Caesars knew it, as Jesus knew of it, was also destroyed. "Would that even today you knew the things that make for peace," he said. That was why he wept. And can anyone who really listens to those words believe that it was only to Jerusalem that he was speaking?

You round the bend in your car, or you circle for a landing in a plane, and there before you or beneath you lies Washington, say, in all its splendor—the Capitol Dome, the Lincoln Memorial, the river—Moscow lies there, San Salvador, Warsaw, Cape Town; and with the missiles in their silos all aimed and ready on both sides of the sea, you don't have to be Jesus to see what he saw. You don't have to be a Christian to shudder two thousand years later at the words he spoke. "Your enemies will dash you to the ground, you and your children within you, and they will not leave one stone upon another." If Jesus had eyes to weep with anymore, there would be tears in them still.

And of course he does have eyes, and the eyes he has are yours and mine.

We speak in terms of defending ourselves, and our enemies speak in the same terms. We must defend ourselves against our enemies as our enemies must defend themselves against us because they are as terrified of us as we are of them and of the unthinkable power each of us has to destroy not only each other but the world itself; and the measures we take to strengthen ourselves against our enemies only increase our enemies' terror and their resolve to strengthen themselves still further against us. The dance of the nations is a dance of death.

The question is, what are we defending, our enemies and we? Well, we are defending our cities and towns. We are defending our homes, our children. We are defending the welfare of our people and the traditions of our fathers. And so of course are they. The tragic irony, of course, is that all these precious things we and our enemies are both defending are threatened by nothing so much as by the very process we use to defend them.

A nation has only so much money to spend, so much time, so much energy, so much ingenuity, to spend, and as the years go by we and our enemies are both spending so much of all of these things on the great instruments of death that we have less and less to spend on the things that make our lives worth even living let alone worth dying for: less and less to spend on hospitals and housing and schools, on feeding our children, on halting the decay of our cities, on works of compassion. We are defending our very lives as nations, we believe, but what happens to the quality of that life, the heart and genius of that life, when such matters as these are neglected? What are we and our enemies doing to defend not just our borders but the only real treasure that lies inside those borders, which is what makes us human and humane as peoples? We preserve such peace as we have by a balance of terror, as we call it —each side so terrified by the other's growing might that neither side dares strike the first blow—but what sort of peace can there be when terror is at the heart of it? And if people say that such talk as this is only preachers' talk, soft-headed, unrealistic, I wonder if anything can be more unrealistic than to suppose that the arsenals of terror that we and our enemies are both amassing won't one day be used; and I wonder if anything can be more unrealistic than to think that once the great weapons are used, there will be any nations, any borders, any cities, any children, any life, any anything left to defend or worth defending.

"Blessed be the King who comes in the name of the Lord," the cry goes up. There is dust in the air with the sun turning it gold. Around a bend in the road, there suddenly is Jerusalem. He draws back on the reins. Crying disfigures his face. "Would that even today you knew the things that make for peace." *Even today,* he says, because there are so few days left. Then the terror of his vision as he looks at the city that is all cities and sees not one stone left standing on another—you and your children within you—your children. "Because you did not know the time of your visitation," he says. Because we don't know who it is who comes to visit us. Because we do not know what he comes to give. The things that make for peace, that is what he comes to give. We do not know these things, he says, and God knows he's right. The absence of peace within our own skins no less than within our nations testifies to that. But we know their names at least. We all of us know in our hearts the holy names of the things that make for peace—real peace—only for once let us honor them by not naming them. Let us name instead only him who is himself the Prince of Peace.

"He shall judge between the nations and shall decide for many peoples; and they shall beat their swords into plowshares and their spears into pruning hooks; nation shall not lift up sword against nation, neither shall they learn war any more." That is our Palm Sunday hope, and it is our only hope. That is what the palms and the shouting are all about. That is what all our singing and worshiping and preaching and praying are all about if they are about anything that matters. The hope that finally by the grace of God the impossible will happen. The hope that Pilate will take him by one hand and Caiaphas by the other, and the Roman soldiers will throw down their spears and the Sanhedrin will bow their heads. The hope that by the power of the Holy Spirit, by the love of Christ, who is Lord of the impossible, the leaders of the enemy nations will draw back, while there is still time for drawing back, from a vision too terrible to name. The hope that you and I also, each in our own puny but crucial way, will work and witness and pray for the things that make for peace, true peace, both in our own lives and in the life of this land.

Despair and hope. They travel the road to Jerusalem together, as together they travel every road we take— despair at what in our madness we are bringing down on our own heads and hope in him who travels the road with us and for us and who is the only one of us all who is not mad. Hope in the King who approaches every human heart like a city. And it is a very great hope as hopes go and well worth all our singing and dancing and sad little palms because not even death can prevail against this King and not even the end of the world, when end it does, will be the end of him and of the mystery and majesty of his love. Blessed be he.

9. Air for Two Voices

JOHN 1:1–16

In the beginning was the Word, and the Word was with God, and the Word was God. He was in the beginning with God; all things were made through him, and without him was not anything made that was made. In him was life, and the life was the light of men. The light shines in the darkness, and the darkness has not overcome it. There was a man sent from God, whose name was John. He came for testimony, to bear witness to the light, that all might believe through him. He was not the light, but came to bear witness to the light. The true light that enlightens every man was coming into the world. He was in the world, and the world was made through him, and yet the world knew him not. He came to his own home, and his own people received him not. But to all who received him, who believed in his name, he gave power to become children of God; who were born not of blood nor of the will of the flesh nor of the will of man, but of God. And the word became flesh and dwelt among us, full of grace and truth; we have beheld his glory, glory as of the only Son from the Father. (John bore witness to him, and cried, "This was he of whom I said, 'He who comes after me ranks before me, for he was before me.' ") And from his fullness we have all received, grace upon grace.

There are two voices in this extraordinary text from John. The first of them is a voice chanting, a cantor's voice, a muezzin's voice, a poet's voice, a choirboy's voice before it has changed—ghostly, virginal, remote and cool as stone. "In the beginning was the Word, and the Word was with God, and the Word was God. He was in the beginning with God." It is sung not said, a hymn not a homily. It is a hymn to perform surgery with, a heart-transplanting voice.

The second voice is insistent and overearnest, a little nasal. It is a voice that wants to make sure, a voice that's trying hard to get everything straight. It is above all a down-to-earth voice. It keeps interrupting. This troublesome confusion about just who the Messiah was, the second voice says: Not John the Baptist certainly, whatever may have been rumored in certain circles. It is a point that cannot be made too clearly or too emphatically. It was not the Baptist. It was Jesus. Right from the beginning Jesus was without any question who it was.

"In him was life, and the life was the light of men. The light shines in darkness, and the darkness has not overcome it," the first voice sings far above all sublunary distinctions, the great Logos hymn.

And then the second voice again. Yes, it says. Only to come back to the Baptist for a moment. He came for testimony, to bear witness to the light. He was not the light but came to bear *witness* to the light, the perspiration beading out on the upper lip, the knuckles whitening.

"And the Word became flesh and dwelt among us," the cry soars up to the great rose window, toward the Pleiades, the battlements of jasper and topaz and amethyst: *"In principio erat verbum* and dwelt among us, full of grace and truth."

And that is true, says the second voice. The Baptist made it absolutely clear when he said—I remember the very words he used—"He who comes after me ranks before me, for he was before me." The Baptist said so himself.

It is good to have both the voices. The sound the

second voice makes is a very human sound, and you need a very human sound to get your bearings by in the midst of the first voice's unearthly music. It is also good to have the interruptions. There should be interruptions in sermons too: the sound of a baby crying, a toilet being flushed —something to remind us of just what this flesh is that the Word became, the Word that was with God, that was God. What it smells and sounds and tastes like, this flesh the Word buckled on like battle dress. When the host is being raised before the altar to the tinkling of bells, it is very meet and right if not his bounden duty for the sexton to walk through with the vacuum cleaner. The New Testament itself is written that way: the risen Christ coming back at dawn to the Sea of Tiberias, Jesus with the mystery of life and death upon him, standing there on the beach saying, "Have you any fish?"

Have you any *fish,* for Christ's sweet sake! Precisely that. The Christ and the chowder. The Messiah and the mackerel. The Word and the flesh. The first voice and the second voice. It is what the great text is all about, of course, this mystery, this tension and scandal; and the text itself, with this antiphony of voices, is its own illustration.

Somebody has to do the vacuuming. Somebody has to keep the accounts and put out the cat. And we are grateful for these things to the second voice which is also of course our own voice, puny and inexhaustible as Faulkner said. It is a human voice. It is the only voice the universe has for speaking of itself and to itself. It is a voice with its own message, its own mystery, and it is important to be told that it was not the Baptist, it was Jesus—not that one standing over there bony and strident in the Jordan, but this one with the queer north country accent, full of grace and truth. Behold, the Baptist said, that is the lamb of God. Not this one but *that* one. We need to know.

But it is the first voice that prevails here, and the first voice that haunts and humbles us—muezzin, cantor, Christ Church chorister—and it is a voice that haunts us at first less with what it means than with how it sounds, with the music before the message, whatever the message is; with the cadences and chords, the silences. *"Im Anfang war das Wort, und das Wort war bei Gott, und Gott war das Wort,"* the first voice incants, *"et omnia per ipsum facta sunt, et sine ipso factum est nihil quod factum est."* It hardly matters what it means at first. *"Et la Parole a été faite chair, et elle a habité parmi nous pleine de grâce et de vérité."* It hardly matters what it means any more than it matters what the sound of the surf means, the organ notes winging like trapped birds toward some break in the gothic dusk. "And from this fullness we have all received, grace upon grace, *Gnade um Gnade, gratiam pro gratia.* He was in the world," the voice sings, "yet the world knew him not," and *"Siehe, das ist Gottes Lamm,"* John says, *"qui ôte le péché du monde. Ecce Agnus Dei qui tollit peccatum mundi.* Behold, the Lamb of God, which taketh away the sin of the world."

Shout "Fire!" Cry "Havoc!" Cry "Help" or "Hallelujah, Hosanna!" A siren in the night. A trumpet at sun-up. A woman singing in the rain, or a man—singing, or weeping, or yelling bloody murder. When you hear it, what happens is that the pulse quickens. It is the sound simply that stirs the heart, literally as well as figuratively stirs it. The sound of the word sung or shouted, its music, literally as well as figuratively stirs it. The sound of the word sung or shouted, its music, literally makes the heart beat faster, makes the blood run quicker and hotter, which is to say the word stirs life. Whatever it is at the level of meaning, at the level of sound, rhythm, breath, the word has the power to stir life. And again this is both what John is saying here and what with his own words he is illustrating: that the Word stirs life even as his own words stir life, stir something. It is hard to hear this prologue read in any tongue without something inside quickening.

The Word becomes flesh. As the word of terror in the night makes the flesh crawl, as the word of desire makes the flesh burn, as other words make the scalp run cold and set the feet running, in maybe some such way this Logos Word of God becomes flesh, becomes Jesus. Jesus so responds to this Word which is God's that he himself becomes the Word, as simple and as complicated as that.

Things get into the air, we say—violence gets into the air, or hate, or panic, or joy—and we catch these things from the air or get caught up in them to the point where the violence or the joy become ours or we theirs. The Word becoming flesh means something like that maybe. God was in the air, and Jesus got so caught up, let this Word of God that was in the air get so under his skin, so in his hair, took it so to heart what there was of God in the air that what was in the air became who he was. He opened his mouth to answer the Word, and like air it filled his mouth.

Or God is poet, say, searching for the right word. Tries Noah, but Noah is a drinking man, and tries Abraham, but Abraham is a little too Mesopotamian with all those wives and whiskers. Tries Moses, but Moses himself is trying too hard; and David too handsome for his own good; Elisha, who sicks the bears on the children. Tries John the Baptist with his locusts and honey, who might almost have worked except for something small but crucial like a sense of the ridiculous or a balanced diet.

Word after word God tries and then finally tries once more to say it right, to get it all into one final Word what he is and what human is and why the suffering of love is precious and how the peace of God is a tiger in the blood. And the Word that God finds—who could have guessed it?—is this one, Jesus of Nazareth, all of it coming alive at last in this life, Jesus this implausible Jew, the Word made finally flesh in Jesus' flesh. Jesus as the *mot juste* of God.

The poetry of the first voice fleshed out in the prose of the second. The Word becoming flesh and dwelling among us full of grace and truth, and that is not all that being flesh involves being full of, so full of that too, like the rest of us, and full of beans too, full of baloney—the scandal of the incarnation, the unimaginable *kenosis* and humbling of God. John means certainly no less than this and almost certainly more.

"In the beginning," he says, "was the Word," and although it is a poem he is writing, we assume that he is being more than just poetic. *"In principio,"* he says, and we assume he means no less than what Genesis means with *bereshith,* which is to say "in the beginning" quite literally: before anything yet had been made that was to be made, before whatever it was that happened to make it possible for Being to happen. You can't speak literally about such things, of course, but we assume that he is speaking as seriously as physicists also speak seriously about the possibility at least of a time beyond time before creation happened. At that point where everything was nothing or nothing everything, before the Big Bang banged or the Steady State was stated, when there was no up and no down, no life and no death, no here and no there, at the very beginning, John says, there was this Word which was God and through which all things were made.

The Bible is usually very universal and makes you want to *see* something—some image to imagine it by. "The light shines in the darkness," John says, and maybe you see an agonizing burst of light with the darkness folding back like petals, like hands. But the imagery of John is based rather on sound than on sight. It is a Word you hear breaking through the unimaginable silence—a creating word, a word that calls forth, a word that stirs life and is life because it is God's word, John says, and has God in it as your words have you in them, have in them your breath and spirit and tell of who you are. Light and dark, the visual, occur in space, but sound, this Word spoken, occurs in time and starts time going. "Let there *be*" the Word comes, and then there *is*, Creation *is*. Something *is* where before there was nothing and the morning stars sing together and all the Sons of God shout for joy because sequence has begun, time has begun, a story has begun.

All of which is to say that John will stop at nothing and here at the start of his gospel asks us to believe no less than everything. He asks us to believe that the Word that became flesh, that became flesh like our flesh, that stood there in the moonshine asking "Have you any fish?" was not a last-minute word and not just one word among many words, but was The Word, the primal, cosmic Word in which was life and light. All that God had from the beginning meant was here in this flesh. The secret of life and death was here.

Behold, the Lamb of God which taketh away the sin of the world. The Lamb of God approaches slowly along the river bank. The Baptist sees him coming, and here the second voice interrupts again. Forget all this about the primal, cosmic Word, the second voice says, and about how it was in the beginning. Just watch the one who is approaching—not the Baptist there in the water but the one who is walking toward the Baptist along the edge of the water. *Siehe, das ist Gottes Lamm.* Nothing matters except him. See how the air stirs, bending the rushes in front of him. Watch his face as he picks his way along—nobody else's face. His. Everything that matters is in his face. Everything that matters is in his hands.

In his hands is the meaning and purpose of creation, the first voice says. In his hands is your life, the second voice says. Behold, he taketh away the sins of the world. *Das ist Gottes Lamm.* His foot slips in the mud. The Baptist waits in the water up to his waist. He cannot see yet whether the one who is coming is the One he has been expecting or not. There is mud on the man's hands now where he grabbed out to keep himself from falling. Perhaps the Baptist is afraid—either afraid that the one who is coming won't be the One or afraid that he will be the One.

Mary, the mother, was also afraid—a little afraid when the angel first came with his announcement, but that was the least of it. He had come so quietly, with an Easter lily in his hand. She had been wearing blue Florentine velvet at the time with her hair hanging down her back like a girl's. Sunlight lay on the tiles like a carpet. The angel stood so still that he could have been one of the columns in the loggia where they met. She had trouble hearing what he said and afterwards thought it might have been a dream. It was not until much later that the real terror came. The real terror came when what the angel had told her would happen happened but in a way she could never have dreamed: squatting there in the straw with her thighs wrenched apart and out of her pain dropping into the howling world something that looked like nothing so much as raw beefsteak: which was the one the angel said was to be called Holy, the Son of the Most High: which was the Word fleshed in, of all flesh, hers.

We have reason, all of us, to be among other things afraid. Like the Baptist waiting there in the river, afraid that the one who is coming along the slippery bank is after all not the One who has been awaited for so long; afraid that the one who is coming and who by now has slipped several times more and has got mud all over everything— either he is out of his head or just isn't looking where he's going—afraid that he is simply not the One at all. Afraid that he is not the Word made flesh because there was no Word in the first place and there was no first place either. In the beginning there was nothing much of anything and still isn't if you add up all there is and place it next to all there is not. Afraid that Jesus and the Baptist meet there in the river like Laurel and Hardy, and as the water rises, their derby hats go floating off toward the Dead Sea.

Or, like the Baptist, afraid that the one who is coming *is* the One. Behold the Lamb of God which taketh away . . . all that is going to have to be taken away. The Lamb of God which giveth . . . , God help us, "the power to become children of God," John says. Just suppose for the sake of an admittedly fantastic argument that he *is* the One who is to come, full of grace and truth and all that. Have you ever considered, have I whose trade it is to consider it ever really considered seriously, just what it is that the Lamb of God is going to have to take away?

I mean if I have any inclination at all, or you, to start

being whatever in God's name it means to be "a child of God"—and let's say there is no argument for having such an inclination but let's just suppose that at certain unguarded moments we have it, this inclination to *start* being children of God—have we any idea at all what by the grace of God we are in all likelihood going to have to *stop* being, stop doing, stop having, stop pretending, stop smacking our lips over, stop hating, stop being scared of, stop chasing after till we're blue in the face and sick at the stomach? O God, deliver us from the Lamb of God which taketh away the sin of the world because the sin of the world is our heart's desire, our uniform, our derby hat. O Lamb of God, have mercy upon us. Christ have mercy upon us.

We have reason, all of us, to be afraid as Mary was afraid, squatting in the straw. She was afraid, I suppose, of giving birth, and why shouldn't she have been? It is by all accounts a painful, bloody process at best. We all have reason to be among other things afraid of giving birth: the wrenching and tearing of it; the risk that we will die in giving birth; more than the risk, the certainty, that if there is going to be a birth, there is first going to have to be a kind of death. One way or another, every new life born out of our old life, every flesh through which God speaks his Word, looks a little like raw beefsteak before it's through. If we are not afraid of it, then we do not know what it involves.

We labor to be born. All what little we have in us of holiness labors for breath, strains to be delivered of darkness into light. It is the secret, inner battle of every one of us. And through all our laboring, God also labors: to deliver what is whole in us from what is broken, to deliver what is true in us from what is false, until in the end we reach the measure of the stature of the fullness of Christ, Paul says—until in the end we become Christ ourselves, no less than that: Christs to each other and Christs to God.

No one ever said it was going to be easy to turn a sow's ear into a silk purse. "Be ye perfect, even as your Father in Heaven is perfect," the great voice sings. Be holy. Be healed. Be human. Because the light shines forth in the darkness, giving power to us all to become children of God. But every time that voice rings out, we answer with the voice of our own littleness, our own earthboundness, that such things are too wonderful for us, that the spirit is willing but the flesh is weak, that we can will what is right but cannot bring it about. It is no easy matter to save us when half the time we don't even want to be saved because we are so at home in the darkness which is home. We none of us come to the end of our days with the saving more than a fraction done at best. But, praise God, the end of our days is not the end of us.

"The light shines in the darkness, and the darkness has not overcome it," the great voice calls out; and with this life behind us, we move on through realms of mystery and mercy and new life beyond our power to imagine until at last, through the cloddish and reluctant flesh of all of us, Almighty God of his grace will speak again in a different tongue and to a lesser but unthinkably significant end the word that was once made flesh and dwelt among us, from whose fullness we have all received.

Behold the Lamb of God which taketh away, which giveth.

10. A Little While

LAMENTATIONS 3:19–23, 26–29
Remember my affliction and my bitterness,
the wormwood and the gall!
My soul continually thinks of it
and is bowed down within me.
But this I call to mind,
and therefore I have hope:

The steadfast love of the Lord never ceases,
his mercies never come to an end;
they are new every morning;
great is thy faithfulness.

It is good that one should wait quietly
for the salvation of the Lord.
It is good for a man that he bear
the yoke in his youth.

Let him sit alone in silence
when he has laid it on him;
let him put his mouth in the dust—
there may yet be hope.

JOHN 16:16–25
"A little while, and you will see me no more; again a little
while, and you will see me." Some of his disciples said to one
another, "What is this that he says to us, 'A little while, and
you will not see me, and again a little while, and you will see
me'; and, 'because I go to the Father'?" They said, "What does
he mean by 'a little while'? We do not know what he means."
Jesus knew that they wanted to ask him; so he said to them,
"Is this what you are asking yourselves, what I meant by
saying, 'A little while, and you will not see me, and again a

little while, and you will see me'? Truly, truly, I say to you, you will weep and lament, but the world will rejoice; you will be sorrowful, but your sorrow will turn into joy. When a woman is in travail she has sorrow, because her hour has come; but when she is delivered of the child, she no longer remembers the anguish, for joy that a child is born into the world. So you have sorrow now, but I will see you again and your hearts will rejoice, and no one will take your joy from you. In that day you will ask nothing of me. Truly, truly, I say to you, if you ask anything of the Father, he will give it to you in my name. Hitherto you have asked nothing in my name; ask, and you will receive, that your joy may be full. I have said this to you in figures; the hour is coming when I shall no longer speak to you in figures but tell you plainly of the Father.''

This scene from the last chapters of John's Gospel is written in the form of a dialogue. The scene is set in the kitchen or whatever room it was where this group of sad and frightened men met to eat what every last one of them knew was the last meal they'd ever have a chance to eat together. It was clear to all of them that Jesus' time had come. He had told them as much, and all his words here have a ring of finality to them. He speaks a great deal over this last supper, the way John describes it, as though he is trying to say everything one more time and say it carefully and say it so they won't forget it when he isn't around to say it to them anymore. They knew that Jesus' time had come, and the chances are they were fairly sure their own time had come too. Jesus never made any bones about what following him was going to mean, and they had every reason to know that in the long run his grim fate was also going to be their grim fate. So we have to imagine the dialogue as spoken by men whose mouths were dry with fear and who were not thinking as clearly as they usually did, which in the disciples' case wasn't all that clear at best. They weren't thinkers, the disciples. They were simple men, and at this last supper especially they had other things on their minds, to put it mildly. Their attention wandered. The sound of Jesus' voice was partly drowned out by the thumping of their own hearts. This is part, I suppose, of why the dialogue has among other things a faintly comic ring to it.

Jesus says, "A little while, and you will see me no more; again a little while, and you will see me." His point doesn't seem a very obscure one, and under ordinary circumstances maybe it wouldn't have seemed so to the disciples either, but these are no ordinary circumstances, and they start buzzing around the table. "What do you suppose he means by saying a little while and you will not see me and again a little while and you will see"? And finally one of them comes right out with it and says, "What does he mean by 'a little while'? We do not know what he means" —latching onto that phrase "a little while" as though it is somehow the crux of the whole matter, coming out with that phrase "a little while" like a man coming out of a burning house holding nothing but an empty coathanger. Then Jesus asks, "Is this what you are asking yourselves, what I meant by saying 'A little while, and you will not see me, and again a little while, and you will see me'?" So the whole cumbersome string of words gets strung out no less than three times before they're done until there is a kind of theater-of-the-absurd ring to it which stems partly from the repetition of his words and the rhythm and partly also, of course, from the incongruity of the occasion: this tragic and fear-laden room and these grown men babbling at each other like children, like clowns, over the crumbs of their bread and the dregs of their wine. "We don't know what you mean," they say, when a child would have known what he meant—and then Jesus finally explains it to them, which is where the comedy ends or maybe in a way where it begins: where the comedy of the absurd shades off into high comedy, the kind of comedy so close to tears that you aren't quite sure whether to laugh or to weep.

Think of Jesus as Charlie Chaplin at his greatest and most Chaplinesque maybe when he explains to them what he means at last. He says in effect that what he means by their not seeing him for a while is that he is going to die and they are going to miss him and be very sad, and what he means by their seeing him again is that he is going to come back after a little while and their sadness will be turned to joy. The great confidence in these words of Jesus is like the twirl of a cane and the twitch of a mustache as the little tramp stands there so jaunty and hopeful in his baggy pants while the whole world threatens to fall on him like a pail of water balanced on top of a door.

Then in a sense Jesus explains what he means in another way. He says, "The hour is coming when I shall no longer speak to you in *figures* but tell you plainly of the Father." This time it is as if he is telling them that even when they do see him, they are seeing him only in a partial and ultimately unsatisfactory way, the way the truth is partly seen in a figure for the truth and partly *not* seen in it.

"My love is like a red, red rose," a poet wrote. And what Jesus is telling the disciples is that so far all they have seen in seeing him is the "red, red rose," so when the time comes when they will see him no longer, maybe it won't be as different as they think. After he's gone, they will no longer have him as a hand to hold, a shoulder to lean on, a face to see—and hence the sorrow of it—but just as before all they ever saw was the *red, red rose* of him and not his *my love,* so they will continue to see him in other partial ways and broken images. The whole life and ministry and death of Jesus is in a way a figure of speech for God, a metaphor for the love that was in him; and what Jesus is telling the disciples is that up until now they have seen only the metaphor—the redness, the fragrance, the beauty of the rose. But the time will come when they will see the God in him plainly. The time will come when they will see plainly for themselves his love itself which the rose of his life at its best has only hinted at. Until that time comes, however, the metaphors are all they will have just as in a way the metaphor is all they have ever had.

And of course metaphors are, God knows, all we any of us have of him. We know Jesus only in broken, fragmentary ways. "A little while, and you will see me no more," he said, and it has been many a long year since anybody saw him plain, least of all the likes of you and me. Shadows, echoes, dreams, odd moments in our lives that speak at best ambiguously and brokenly of him—they are the most we have seen of Jesus.

I remember a spring or so ago walking with a friend though a stand of maple trees at sugaring time. The sap buckets were hung from the trees, and if you were quiet, you could hear the sap dripping into them: all through the woods, if you kept still, you could hear the hushed drip-dropping of the sap into a thousand buckets or more hung out in the early spring woods with the sun coming down in long shafts through the trees. The sap of a maple is like rainwater, very soft, and almost without taste except for the faintest tinge of sweetness to it, and when my friend said he'd never tried it, I offered to give him a taste. I had to unhook the bucket from the tap to hold it for him, and when he bent his head to drink from it, I tipped the bucket down to his lips, and just as he was about to take a sip, he looked up at me and said, "I have a feeling you ought to be saying some words."

Well, my friend is no more or less religious than the next person, and we'd been chattering on about nothing in particular as we walked along until just at that moment as I tipped the bucket to his lips, he said what he said, and said it partly as a joke. He had a feeling I should be saying some words, he said, as I tipped the bucket to his lips so he could taste for the first time the taste of the lifeblood of a tree. And of course for a moment those unsaid words fell through the air of those woods like the shafts of sun, and it was no joke because the whole place became another place or became more deeply the place it truly was; and he and I became different, something happened for a second to the air around us and between us. It was not much and lasted only for a moment before it was gone. But it happened—this glimpse of something dimly seen, dimly heard, this sense of something deeply hidden.

One more moment to stand for the kind of moments I mean. A friend of mine who was an historian got talking once about George Washington for some reason and how he'd never known much about Washington or been especially interested to find out more. But he said he'd never forget something he once heard about him. He said he had a great aunt who'd had a grandfather who was in Washington's army from Valley Forge to Yorktown, and my friend told me how once when he was a little boy, the old lady told him something she remembered hearing her grandfather say. She said she'd always remembered his exact words, and what he'd said was, "He was a fine man, General Washington. He was everything a man should be."

Hardly one of the great utterances of our time, but words that came from the lips of someone who'd actually known the man, and my historian friend said that every time he thought of those words, they made his scalp tingle as they made mine tingle a little when he told them to me, because just for a moment they bring George Washington of all people alive a little—not just the face on the one-dollar bill, the Father of his Country carved in marble, but "he was a fine man, General Washington. He was everything a man should be," a man with real blood in his veins; in the eyes of someone who'd seen him and known him as his words come down through an old lady's memory: a *fine* man.

Once in a while things flicker up out of our lives like a flame out of ashes we'd thought were long since dead, and by the flickering we see things, or think we do, that for a second or two make not all the difference in the world to us maybe but enough of a difference to stay in our memory like a good dream. He was a fine man, General Jesus. He was everything a man should be, a God should be—once in a while somebody says it to us who has seen him plain somehow and known him, because there are such people in the world, people whose lives flicker with the life they have seen, and whose words and lives make our scalps tingle, make us believe that there actually was a Jesus once and in some sense still is.

"A little while and you will not see me," Jesus said,

and he means we will not see him except in such broken ways as these—at second hand, from a great distance. Even in church we don't often see him much better than that. Maybe the flame of a candle shows him forth better than a sermon can. Maybe there is more of Jesus in our silences than in our prayers. Maybe he's more fully present in our restlessness to get out into the fresh air again, to get out of church and back to the crazy, holy business of our lives again. If the church is his body in the world, his hands and feet, then all we can say is that his body is at best a broken body. If people like you and me are the only hands he has, then of all men he is most short-handed.

Sunday after Sunday we go to church because we are looking for Jesus in some uncertain way or another—of all the reasons we have, I think this is at the heart of them. We go to church looking for him because not just maple woods and silence and the occasional testimony of his saints speak to us of him, but because the spirit of him is so at large in the air we breathe that almost anything we see can turn into the shadow of him if we're not careful or if we *are* careful—a piece of bread, a glass of wine. We go to church looking for Jesus in some uncertain way because in some uncertain way we have seen him, have seen enough of him to suspect that if there is anyone who can lighten the dimness of us, he is the one who can—the Light of the World; the light, if we could only see him, even of our own dim inner worlds.

Jesus started us looking for him himself, of course. "Inasmuch as ye have done it unto one of the least of these my brethren, ye have done it unto me." He starts us looking for him in the most outlandish places—some bleary wino lurching out of a doorway for a handout, the skinny child crossing the street in the rain, the old man dying of loneliness and boredom in some nursing home we avoid because it is literally as depressing as hell.

"Cleave the wood, and I am there," Jesus says in one of the apocryphal gospels. "Lift up the stone, and I am there." There is no depth of human need where we cannot see him both needing us and reaching out to our need, but at best we see him only dimly. The metaphor in part reveals, in part conceals. The tears we can sometimes shed at the sight of him in our own and others' needs both clear our eyes and also blind our eyes. "I have a feeling you should be saying some words," my friend said to me as I gave him the tree to drink, and in a way the silence said them and in another way it was only silence.

"Truly, truly, I say to you, . . . you will be sorrowful," Jesus said. Well, and we're sorrowful about lots of things, you and I, God knows. It goes with the territory, sorrow. We carry it about with us the way a snail carries its shell; it is one of the homes we live in—sorrow about our country and about our pillaged earth, sorrow that youth grows old and beauty fades. Sorrow about death—about all the undone things the dead leave behind them as we will leave undone things behind us too when our time comes, like a pair of old shoes broken in to take us on some blessed journey we never got around to taking, maybe the most crucial journey of our lives. But as Christians we inherit this special refinement of sorrow that Jesus speaks of, this sorrow for connoisseurs—which is the sorrow of not see-ing plainly the One we need most to see.

I remember a Jewish boy I had in a New Testament class for a while who said one day in a burst of real impa-tience and anger, "Don't you get sick and tired, you Christians, of waiting for someone to come back who never comes back?" And I found myself asking him if to wait for a Christ who never comes back is all that much harder than to wait for a Christ who never comes at all, and in that moment we became brothers as we'd never been before, both of us Jews in the sorrow of our waiting, of our seeing, yes, sometimes a little something, somewhere, but never enough, of seeing but not seeing. The high comedy of it, of not knowing whether to laugh or to weep.

This is the bottom of the long hill that faith has to travel, the deepest part of the valley, which is the valley of the Shadow itself. Nobody knows that valley better in its darkness than the Jew in us all, the part of us all that grows sick with waiting for a Savior to come save. "A little while and you will see me no more." Maybe the disciples were right to latch on to that one naked phrase "a little while" and to make it the cutting edge of their question. "What does he mean by, God help us all, 'a little while,' " they asked with their dry tongues clacking. "A little while" two thousand years long, and they all sit there around the table in their baggy pants with the pail of water teetering on top of the door as they ask about it. How does a man while away "a little while" like that? is the question they're asking, and it's out of the Book of Lamentations that the answer wells up in a marvelous phrase that somehow has all of Scripture in it, all of Jew and Christian both: "Let him put his mouth in the dust," the book says. "There may yet be hope."

In Dostoevski's novel *The Brothers Karamazov* there is an extraordinary scene where the old monk Father Zossima dies. They lay him out in his coffin in the chapel, and all of the monks wait around to see a miracle—for the body to give off the fragrance of a rose, maybe, or his dead face to flicker with a holy light. But no miracle happens, and not only does no miracle happen, but as time goes by something else happens instead. After a while the body shows signs of decomposition, and gradually—though at first the monks try not to notice it—the chapel is filled with the stink of death. No miracle happens, but decay and death happen, the stench of dust returning to dust; and the one who loved the old man most—Alyosha, the youngest of the brothers—stands ready to give the whole thing up as a bad joke, to give up all hope of miracle, to give up his life, to give up if not God himself then the dusty world that hides God from our sight. Then he has this dream.

He is keeping vigil at the old man's coffin while one of the monks reads the story of the Wedding at Cana over it, and when he falls asleep, the dream comes. It is a dream about Cana. There are the guests, there are the young couple sitting, the wise governor of the feast, and suddenly there is old Zossima too—a little thin old man with tiny wrinkles on his face, and of all the things he could be doing, what he is doing in that dream is laughing, laughing at that great feast like a child. And when Alyosha wakes up, he does something that he himself does not fully understand. He tears out of the chapel and rushes down into the monastery yard. He hears inside himself the words, "Water the earth with the tears of your joy and love those tears" and suddenly he gets down on all fours and kisses the earth with his lips; and when he gets up, he's no longer a teary wreck of a boy but a "champion," Dostoevski writes—some kind of crazy champion and hero.

"Let him put his mouth in the dust—there may yet be hope," the prophet of Lamentations writes. We've got to watch out for these prophets and novelists. They are apt to get so carried away by what they're saying that we are in danger of getting carried away with them—picture sober, clear-headed people like you and me making clowns of ourselves by getting down on all fours in our Sunday-go-to-meeting best, our baggy pants, and kissing the mucked up sod. And Jesus says it too in a way—looks at those twelve comedians sitting around the table shaking in their boots and weeping into their beer, looks at us, and says, "You will be sorrowful, but your sorrow will turn into joy."

What do they really mean if they mean anything real at all, aren't just carried away by their own good dreams and the power of their own poetry? Maybe we have to put our mouths to the dust and kiss it ourselves to know. Jesus explains with a metaphor again, he who is himself a kind of metaphor as we dimly see him: his beloved, our beloved, like a red, red rose, like him. He says, "When a woman is in travail, she has sorrow because her time has come; but when she is delivered of the child, she no longer remembers the anguish, for joy that a child has been born into the world." And the Greek word *anthropos* doesn't mean *child* but means *human being,* so what Jesus is saying is that we no longer remember the anguish for joy that a *human being* has been born into the world, and the human being that is born is of course ourselves.

I wonder if there is any one of us who does not at least faintly see what he means. There is a kind of high comedy about our faith. There is a kind of high comedy about seeing and not seeing, about waiting, about being human but not quite human. We wait for him to come—more than we know, each of us waits for our heart's desire—and he comes only in metaphors, in shadowy glimpses through the tall and bleeding trees; in long silences through which some words should be spoken and are spoken but never quite audibly enough for us to be sure we've heard them right: "The blood of our Lord Jesus Christ which was shed for thee preserve thy body and soul unto everlasting life."

Body and soul, we wait for new life to make us everlastingly alive, new blood to flow through our dusty and sorrowing world, soft as rainwater and almost without taste but with the faintest tinge of sweetness to it. He was a fine man, our Lord and General. He was everything a man should be. He was everything we all should be and from the deepest part of ourselves yearn to be—loving, brave, just—but are not yet, not by a long shot.

You hardly know whether to laugh or to weep. Well, laugh then, since you have to choose one or the other. Laugh like the wrinkled old man in the dream with the knowledge that there may yet be hope not just beyond the dust of our world but within the dust. His very absence here in the dust speaks of his presence. Our very brokenness here speaks of wholeness and holiness. The emptiness we carry around inside us through the dust whispers like a seashell of the great sea that it belongs to and that belongs to it. "I have said this to you in figures," Jesus says, but "the hour is coming when I shall no longer speak to you in figures but tell you plainly of the Father." This is his promise, and watering the earth with the tears of our joy, we make it our laughter and our prayer.

11. Deliverance

DEUTERONOMY 26:5-9

"And you shall make response before the Lord your God, 'A wandering Aramean was my father; and he went down into Egypt and sojourned there, few in number; and there we became a nation, great, mighty, and populous. And the Egyptians treated us harshly, and afflicted us, and laid upon us hard bondage. Then we cried to the Lord the God of our fathers, and the Lord heard our voice, and saw our affliction, our toil, and our oppression; and the Lord brought us out of Egypt with a mighty hand and an outstretched arm, with great terror, with signs and wonders; and he brought us into this place and gave us this land, a land flowing with milk and honey.' "

MATTHEW 11:28-30

Come to me, all you who labor and are heavy laden, and I will give you rest. Take my yoke upon you and learn from me; for I am gentle and lowly of heart, and you will find rest for your souls. For my yoke is easy, and my burden is light.

The words inscribed on the Statue of Liberty where it stands on Bedloe's Island in New York harbor are familiar to all of us:

> Give me your tired, your poor,
> Your huddled masses yearning to be free,
> The wretched refuse of your teeming shore.
> Send these, the homeless, tempest-tossed, to me;
> I lift my torch beside the golden door.

It is not great poetry, perhaps, and many a cynical word could be spoken about how the golden door that the goddess of liberty lights with her torch turned out for many to be the door to a wretchedness greater than any they had left behind on the teeming shores of their homelands. But nevertheless I think the old words have power in them still, if we let them, to move us, to touch us close to where we live. And the reason they have such power, I believe, is that one way or another they are words about us. Whether we're rich or poor, whether our forebears came to this country on the Mayflower or a New England slave ship or a nineteenth-century clipper or in a twentieth-century jet, those huddled masses are part of who all of us are, both as individuals and as a people. They are our fathers and mothers. They are our common past. Yet it goes farther and deeper than that. They are our past, and yet they are also ourselves. In countless ways, both hidden and not so hidden, it is you and I who are the homeless and tempest-tossed, waiting on our own Ellis Islands for the great promise to be kept of a new world, a new life, which we haven't yet found. We are the ones who yearn to breathe free. We stand not merely like them but in a sense with them beside the golden door. To read the story of our immigrant forebears as it is summarized on the base of the old statue is to read our own story, and maybe it is only when we see that it is our own story that we can really understand either it or ourselves.

And so I think it is with the stories of Scripture—all those ancient tales that are apt to seem so worn out and remote and that we've heard so many times that they tend to go threadbare like old stage sets, so familiar that when they're read aloud to us in church we hardly even hear them. But a wandering Aramean was also our father, or a wandering Englishman, a wandering Jew or German or Chinese, and the stories about them are also stories about our fathers and mothers—the Old Testament stories about Sarah and Abraham, about David and Deborah, about the glory of Solomon and the fall of Jerusalem—and of course the Gospel stories too, which are so much smaller in their way, so much quieter, but belong even more especially to us and tend even more nearly to touch us where we live: Jesus goes out in a boat and a storm comes up; Mary Magdalen stands weeping outside the deserted tomb. The stories of Scripture are stories about where we come from and where we are going as much as the story of our immigrant past is; and here too, if we are to understand what they mean—what they mean to us, mean for us, mean about us—we have to try to get inside them somehow. Through whatever imagination, intuition, human compassion we can muster, we have to stand where these people stood and feel what they felt: to sail in that little boat as the wind freshened and the waves started to heave; to bury our own faces in our hands before the terrible darkness of that tomb or the sight of that great city being laid waste.

And maybe this is nowhere truer than with the one story out of which in a sense all the other stories come, which is the story summarized in Deuteronomy 26:5–9. It is the story of how some four thousand years ago or whatever a pack of ragged Hebrew slaves escaped from bondage in the Egypt of the pharaohs. It is the story of how Israel first entered history as a people which still remains a people to this day when all the other peoples of the ancient Near East have long since lost their original identities, their great cities long since fallen into ruin and their mighty gods with them. It is the story of the birth of

Israel's faith, out of which comes our faith. It is the story of the journey that lies ahead of us with all its dangers and longings, with all its high and holy hopes.

"The Egyptians treated us harshly, and afflicted us, and laid upon us hard bondage," Deuteronomy says. "Then we cried to the Lord the God of our fathers, and the Lord heard our voice, and saw our affliction . . . and brought us out of Egypt with a mighty hand . . . and gave us this land." This land. Gave it to us. At least we got here somehow, ragged pack that we are, the wandering children of wanderers, all of us. But even though we got here, does it take a preacher to tell us that much of the oppression and affliction are still ours? That we remain the homeless and tempest-tossed even though in some sense this land is home? After the Exodus, the children of Israel still had the wilderness to face, and so do we. The past is always a living part of the present, even a past too distant to imagine. The Exodus is always happening, the wilderness is always happening, and that is why the lines on the statue speak of it no less than the lines in the Scriptures, no less than the lines in our own faces. In many ways the hard bondage is still ours, and yet the deliverance is ours too, the Exodus is ours. To be a Christian must mean at least that, I think —means that though, God knows, the truth of Christ has not yet set us free to be Christs, to be true, ourselves, at least we have glimpsed that truth—at some point in the past each of us embraced it with something like passion, were embraced by it. That is why we're here for Christ's sake. That is where our faith comes from or came from once. The Lord brought us out with a mighty hand. We all have our own strange tales to tell. We wait on the far shore of the Sea of Reeds with the chariots of pharaoh awash behind us. We wait on Ellis Island with all that we have, all that we are, strapped to our backs. We wait wherever it is that we wait as the fierce wind blows. With our faces buried in our hands, we stand before the golden door.

What is it like to be a slave? We've all seen reconstructions of the building of the pyramids, the anonymous little dark-skinned figures laboring up ramps like Sisyphus to heave the great stones into place. But the Bible doesn't call us primarily to reconstruct the past. "The Lord heard *our* voice," it says. That is the voice we're called to listen to here, the voice of our own slavery. Is it true that we're slaves? Can we be slaves, we who of all people are so much our own masters? And the answer, of course, is that we're slaves precisely because we are our own masters.

The Free World, we call it. We have no pharaoh, no ayatollah, no military strongman to oppress us. We have a government of our own choosing to represent us among the nations and to do our will. But for years now the governments we've chosen, and the governments of the nations we call our enemies, have been locked, for what both sides believe to be the best of reasons, in a cold and bloodless war which we're told even little children these days lie awake in their beds knowing could any day— while they're driving to school or eating lunch or throwing a Frisbie—turn into a war so hot and bloody that no sane person could possibly will it and that would be the fiery, six-star spectacular end of civilization on this planet. We know this as surely as we know anything, all of us know it, and yet our voices are so weak, our information so fragmentary, our power to act so limited, that there is little we can do except wait like little children ourselves to see whether the grown-ups decide for life or for death. And to live like that, to live with our own destinies so much out of our control, not to mention the destiny of everything and everybody else we hold dear, is part at least, I can only suppose, of what it means to live as a slave.

There are other ways of describing that slavery. To the degree that we're more or less compassionate, more or less rational, more or less human, to the degree that underneath it all we are by and large lovers of peace, of decency, after a fashion lovers even of each other, we live in many ways like strangers and exiles in our own land—not just appalled at the power we have given into the hands of our political leaders but appalled too by the culture we have created. It seems to me that if history lasts long enough for archaeologists some five hundred or a thousand years hence, say, to dig back into our age, I predict they will be stunned by what they discover. I picture them in their beards and pith helmets unearthing the movies and plays and television we watched, poring over the books we read, the art we created, the kind of black comedy we laughed at, and the kind of horrors that fascinated us on the evening news. Violence without motive. Darkness without escape. Sex without love or beauty. The criminal, the monstrous, the demonic, the psychopathic. I picture them staggered to discover how obsessed we were with the very madness that destroyed us.

Of course the trouble with naming our madness in a sermon like this is that it encourages people like you and me to believe that we somehow stand apart from it, whereas needless to say the truth of the matter is that we stand, like everybody else, up to our necks in it, if only in the sense that we take it as much for granted as earlier ages took human sacrifice for granted, or literal slavery, or the death camps of Andersonville or the Third Reich. And the other trouble with it is that we're apt to feel that simply by naming and deploring our madness we have done all that we can be expected to do about it until the next time somebody names it to us when we will of course deplore it again. But if we're honest we must name it anyway. Rock music. Hard rock, acid rock, punk rock. No-future rock as I'm told yet another form of it is called. It is the music our age stands to be remembered by if there are any to remember it—the endlessly repetitious, superamplified, agonized howl of an age for whom this world for all its great beauty can never feel like home because at any moment it may blow up in our faces like a trick cigar.

We are captives in the house we have built for ourselves, which is in many ways a haunted house—a house haunted, a world haunted, by the dark spirits we ourselves have raised—and to see it for what it is, even as little as we do, is to feel as estranged as slaves must feel in the place of their captivity. It is to feel, inside our own lives, as helpless to escape as slaves are helpless, because of course the one thing we can't escape is ourselves.

Ourselves. You and I. We can escape a little from time to time. We can leave the newspaper unread, the tube turned off. We can get away someplace for a day or two or have an extra drink before supper. But we can't get away from who we are because that is something we carry around like the bedrolls our ancestors lugged off the boat the day somebody tried to sell them the Brooklyn Bridge or dragged across the Sea of Reeds with those chariots hot on their weary tails. We've had our good times surely, our blessed times. All of us have. We've loved a few people truly here and there along the way, and here and there along the way, with any luck at all, we've been loved truly in return. There have been moments when we've been braver and wiser and kinder than we thought we knew how to be. Every once and a while a word was spoken that gave us back our lives again; maybe we even spoke such a word ourselves. On the scale of nations, more than once we have seen a terrible war give way to at least a precarious peace, and beggars can't be choosers. Maybe civilization will squeak through after all. But real peace? What it must be like to be truly free?

Now and then we've had our visions of it, thank God —of the people we might be, that at our best we sometimes dream of being. Here and there we've heard echoes of what our lives together could be—as humans, as nations —if only we lived them right. Suppose we could step out, for keeps, from everything in the past that weighs us down and holds us back like the great stones of the pyramid builders—the things we've done or failed to do that deaden, wreck, cripple. Suppose we could cast off once and for all every nightmare we can imagine about the future and for once in our lives live just in the mystery and gift of today. Suppose that for once we could lose ourselves—the way when you're in love you can lose yourself —in the sheer delight of each other's presence, in the outlandish and wonderful differences between us no less than in all we have in common—capitalist and communist, black and white, old and young, homosexual and heterosexual, swinger and square, male and female. To dream such a dream as that is all but to weep because in one way it seems so almost possible, so only just barely out of reach, and in other ways farther away than the farthest star. As men and women, a nation, a world, we're so enslaved by all the old patterns of fear and self-seeking, self-doubt, self-torment, so shackled by old habits of indifference that we don't know how to get the hell out, which is much of what hell means in the first place: hell as the place you can't get out of.

Exodus is getting the hell out. Exodus means getting the hell out of all that is homicidal and suicidal about this world that we're both trapped in and that's trapped in us. It means getting the hell out of hell. And Exodus means there is a way out. There is deliverance, to use that beautiful old word, and Christians are people who through such now-and-then, here-and-there visions as they've had, through Christ, have been delivered just enough to know that there's more where that came from, and whose experience of the little deliverance that has already happened inside themselves and whose faith in the deliverance still to happen is what sees them through the night.

"He descended into hell," the Apostles' Creed says in language that reeks of mythology and yet in a way is maybe truer to life as we know it than any other words the creed contains. It is because Christ descends and is always descending into hell that we, who much of the time live in its suburbs, know him to the degree that we know him at all. He is our Moses and the mighty hand that drives back the waters of the sea. He is our Exodus. He is himself the golden door to home before which we all of us stand in our homelessness.

It is so easy to say it in a way that makes it beautiful, that makes it moving, but so hard to say it in a way that makes it real, that makes it happen. We have heard it so much and listened to it so little. Christ is the way. The way out. The way home. The only way that matters. A preacher like me travels three thousand miles to say it—a preposterous thing to do. Yet if what the preacher travels to say just happens to be true, then no price is too preposterous. How does a preacher, how does anybody, say it right?

"Come to me," is how Christ himself says it. The words are as fresh as air is fresh, as clear as water, as unpoetic as bread. It is in ourselves that the poetry must happen if it happens at all. "All you who labor," he says, all of us who have been delivered just enough to know that we labor still. "Take my yoke upon you." We are to lay down our own yokes, whatever they happen to be. Who knows them better than you and I know them? The staleness, the sadness, the servitude of never being more than who we've always been. "And I will give you rest," he says—and a very curious kind of rest it is because the way Christ is, of course, is not a way of escaping the world but of loving the world for the beauty it has, beneath all the horror, of being loved by him.

We are to come to him even though the world calls us in a hundred different directions. We are to be fools for his sake. We are to take risks for him and be merry for him. We are to work for peace and pray for miracles. We are to go places and do things and speak words that, without him, we wouldn't even dare dream of. We know so much more than we ever let on about what he would have each of us do in our own lives—what door to open, what hand to take. We have within us, each one, so much more of his power than we ever spend—such misers of miracle we are, such pinchpenny guardians of grace.

If we have a long way to go, God knows we have also come a long way. Through hell and high water we have been delivered as far as this day, this place, with faith maybe not much bigger than a mustard seed but having it on highest authority that that is faith enough. O Thou who makest even hell thy habitation and who partest the high waters with thy mighty hand, deliver our world. Deliver us.

12. Dereliction

PSALM 74:1–16 passim

O God, why dost thou cast us off forever? Why does thy anger
smoke against the sheep of thy pasture? Remember thy congregation, which thou hast gotten of old, . . . Direct thy steps
to the perpetual ruins; the enemy has destroyed everything in
the sanctuary! Thy foes have roared in the midst of thy holy
place; . . . At the upper entrance they hacked the wooden
trellis with axes. And then all its carved wood they broke down
with hatchets and hammers. They set thy sanctuary on fire; to
the ground they desecrated the dwelling place of thy name.
. . . We do not see our signs; there is no longer any prophet,
and there is none among us who knows how long. . . . Yet God
my King is from of old, working salvation in the midst of the
earth. . . . Thine is the day, thine also is the night.

JOHN 16:7, 8

Nevertheless I tell you the truth; it is to your advantage that
I go away, for if I do not go away, the Counselor will not come
to you; but if I go, I will send him to you. And when he comes,
he will convince the world of sin and of righteousness and of
judgment.

According to the Book of Kings, it was "in the fifth month,
on the seventh day of the month—which was the nine-
teenth year of King Nebuchadnezzar, king of Babylon"
that the Babylonian forces entered Jerusalem and, among
other things, destroyed the great Temple of Solomon in

all its glory. "At the upper entrance they hacked the wooden trellis with axes," says the Seventy-fourth Psalm, "all its carved wood they broke down with hatchets and hammers. They set thy sanctuary on fire." You can all but hear the chaos and din of it—the falling masonry and splintering wood, the massive cedar beams overlaid with gold thundering to the floor, the crackle and hiss of flames as they swept up the walls all carved with pomegranates, palm trees, lilies, as they feathered with fire the great olivewood cherubim with their outstretched wings. Who can ever forget it—the burning embers floating through the sky and the terrible heat of it as the priests scattered before it like dead leaves before the wind?

"To the ground they desecrated the dwelling place of thy name," says this horror-struck psalm. "The enemy has destroyed everything in the sanctuary! Thy foes have roared in the midst of thy holy place." And that of course was close to the worst of it: that the place which was destroyed was not just the pride and glory of Jerusalem but was also God's place. They didn't exactly say it was the place where God dwelled because at its wisest Israel always stopped just short of saying that God dwelled anywhere in space, but it was the place where God tabernacled at least, where he pitched his tent, camped out, to hear prayer and accept sacrifice, the place where his secret name was spoken and heard, where his glory was at least glimpsed as Isaiah had glimpsed it in the year when King Uzziah died. So of all places anywhere, the Temple was the holiest place. If God made himself known anyplace, that was where he did it. And now that place was a shambles, a smouldering ruin, an unholy mess.

There are many things you could say about it, and one

of them is simply that King Nebuchadnezzar put King Yahweh to rout and took his Temple the way Grant took Richmond. You could say that when it came to a direct confrontation, not even God in his holiness was a match for Babylonians in their might with their hatchets and axes and flaming torches. You could say, if you dared to say it, that God is only a dream, a shadow, a word, whereas hatchets are solid and real the way Babylonians and bombs are real; and that on the day when this whole planet is finally chopped down, burned up, the dream of God will vanish with it as surely as the Temple did on the fifth day of the seventh month with King Nebuchadnezzar standing by at the hotline to get the good news. That is one thing you could say, and my own guess is that there were probably more than a few in Jerusalem who were saying it in 586 B.C. just as there are more than a few who are saying it today. Nebuchadnezzar routed God because God is of no substance and reality in himself, and thus eminently routable. Nebuchadnezzar was able to dispose of God and his Temple, both, with comparative ease because God, if he had ever existed at all, was dead and gone before Nebuchadnezzar got there.

But needless to say, that was not what the prophets were saying. What the prophets were saying was that the reason Nebuchadnezzar was able to destroy the Temple of God in all its holiness was that God had long since left the Temple to its fate in anger and despair and taken his holiness with him. The prophet Jeremiah went and stood right in the court of the Temple itself on the eve of its destruction and said it—in the terrible candor of his calling blurted it out with such force that his eyes bulged in their sockets: "Do not trust in these deceptive words: 'This is the Temple of the Lord, the Temple of the Lord, the Temple of the Lord.' " He shouted it three times in a row so nobody would miss it. And then he spoke what he believed was the word of God himself: "Will you steal, murder, commit adultery, swear falsely, . . . go after other Gods . . . and then come before me in this house, which is called by my name, and say, 'We are delivered'?" For Jeremiah, in other words, the Temple fell to the Babylonians like a house of cards not because God was a pushover but because a house of cards was what God's people had made of it.

"We are delivered," they said in their Temple while it was still in business. They had been delivered at the Exodus and many a time since. They had left behind them in Egypt the worst bondage of all which was bondage to themselves. They had been shown the way to get the hell out, but they were still in hell because by letting their faith become mainly a matter of ritual and busyness inside the Temple and by living their lives outside the Temple as though there was no God at all to give a hang how they lived them and thus was really no God at all, hell was what they had made for themselves and within themselves. It was they themselves who had desecrated the Temple, Jeremiah said, and the Babylonians had only delivered the coup de grâce. Now they were on their own. God was no longer to be found where for centuries they had expected to find him. And the Seventy-fourth Psalm begins like a dog howling at the moon: "O God, why dost thou cast us off for ever? . . . Remember thy congregation, which thou hast gotten of old." But as far as the Psalmist can tell, God did not remember them. "We do not see our signs," he says. "There is no longer any prophet, and there is none among us who knows how long." That was the worst of it all. The people of the Exodus, the people who had been delivered, were lost, and their cry is a cry of dereliction that even after two and a half thousand years has still such a ring of reality to it that it is hard to hear it and remain unmoved, hard to think of it as having mere historical interest. "O God, why dost thou cast us off?" Is there anyone who has not only heard that cry but at times also cried it?

There is a restaurant in a city somewhere, a sort of quick-lunch place with no tablecloths on the tables, just the ketchup and mustard jars on the bare wood. It seems to be raining outside. An elderly man with a raincoat and umbrella has turned at the door. Another man glances up as he sits there smoking a cigar over a newspaper and the remains of his coffee. Two teenagers sit at a table, one of them with a cigarette in his mouth. They are all looking at the same thing, which is an old woman and a small boy who are sharing a table with the teenagers. Their heads are bowed. They are saying grace. The people watching them watch with dazed fascination. The small boy's ears stick out from his head like the handles of a jug. The old woman's eyes are closed, her hair untidy under a hat that has seen better days. The people are watching something that you feel they may have been part of once but are part of no longer. Through the plate-glass window and the rain, the city looks dim, monotonous, industrial. The old woman and the boy are saying grace there, and for a moment the silence in the place is fathomless. The watchers are watching something that they've all but forgotten and will probably forget again as soon as the moment passes. They could be watching creatures from another planet. The old woman and the boy in their old-fashioned clothes, praying their old-fashioned prayer, are leftovers from a day that has long since ceased to be.

It is not fashionable to praise Norman Rockwell over-much, that old master of nostalgia and American corn, but we have to praise him at least for this most haunting and maybe most enduring of all his *Saturday Evening Post* cov-ers which touches on something that I think touches us all. It was some thirty years ago that he painted it, but the likeness remains fresh and true to this day, and of course it is a likeness of us and of a world not unlike the one the Seventy-fourth Psalm describes.

For us the Temple still stands, to be sure. The great cathedrals still stand. The churches still stand, big ones and little ones, some that are almost full every Sunday and others that are almost empty. The Church is still in busi-ness, in other words, but the question is, what is that business, what goes on in these strange buildings scattered thick over the surface of the earth? Why do people con-tinue to go there? What do they find when they get there? What do they fail to find? Why do people go to them no longer? Fundamentalists, liberals, evangelicals, humanists, charismatics, Roman Catholics, Jehovah's Witnesses—are all of them doing the same thing or are they doing differ-ent things? Are some of them doing it right and others doing it wrong? Is there any sense in which you can say that God is present in any of them or all of them? These are not rhetorical questions, questions whose answers I plan to pull out of the hat at the end of my sermon. It's because I don't know the answers that I'm asking them both of you and of myself. And it's because some of you may share my confusion and uncertainty that it seems crucial to ask them also of God. Maybe at least part of our business in a church is to ask what is going on in it. Is there anything more or less important, real, holy, going on there than anyplace else?

As a church we have not been demolished with hatchets and axes and torches, and the foes of God have not roared in our sanctuary except insofar as from time to time you and I are his foes. The church is intact. The plumbing and furnace work, at least most of the time. The Sunday School rooms are clean and adequately lit. The bills are paid. The ministers by and large earn their keep. Sermons are preached, the young are baptized and married, the old buried. The sick and lonely are visited, and the poor remembered, and the congregation more or less does its share too. The wine is poured and the bread eaten over and over again. "Drink this, eat this, in remembrance of me," and he is remembered here, and we come to remember and be remembered. We pray. We worship. Sometimes we even open our hearts a little to the one who promises to lead us out, to deliver us, and who has delivered us at least as far as this place itself where with such faith as we have, we sometimes yearn above all things for full deliverance and sometimes, I suspect, would turn it down cold if the chance came because with part of ourselves we cling to things as they are even when they are killing us and we are far from eager to find out what full deliverance might mean.

The church is intact in many ways, and at their best most of the things the church does serve their purpose— sometimes, we pray, serve even Christ's purpose—and at their worst are probably at least harmless. But is it possible that something crucial is missing the way something crucial was missing in the Temple at Jerusalem in 586 B.C., which is why it fell like a ton of bricks? "You are the body of Christ," Paul said, and if you stop to think of it at all, that is a most fateful and devastating word. Christ on this earth was the healer of the sick, the feeder of the hungry, the hope of the hopeless, the sinners' friend, and thank God for that because that means he is also our hope, our friend. Thank God for every time the church remembers that and acts out of that.

But Christ was also a tiger, the denouncer of a narrow and loveless piety, the scourge of the merely moral, the enemy of every religious tradition of his day, no matter how sacred, that did not serve the Kingdom as he saw it and embodied it in all its wildness and beauty. Where he was, passion was, life was. To be near him was to catch life from him the way sails catch the wind. He was the Prince of Peace, and when he said, "I have not come to bring peace, but a sword," what he presumably meant was that it was not peacefulness and passivity that he came to bring but that high and life-breathing peace that burns at the hearts only of those who are willing to do battle, as he did battle, to bring to pass God's loving, healing, forgiving will for the world and all its people.

In these ways too the church is called, you and I are called, to be Christ's body, to be life-givers, and when I think of that, I think of a New England college where I preach from time to time in a vast Gothic chapel that is used only once or twice a year and the rest of the time stands empty. And I remember how the last time I was there and looked out into all that great vaulted space which month after month is full of nothing but shadows, it struck me as saying much what the Rockwell cover is saying. The other people in the restaurant look with dazed astonishment at the old woman and the small boy at their prayers because something seems to be alive and real inside them in that unlikely place, something that in many a place where you would expect to find it seems scarcely alive at all. Even when churches are full to overflowing, it is often hard not to sense an inner emptiness as great as the emptiness of that college chapel—the sense that though the great feast is still in progress and many of the guests still in their seats, the heart has somehow gone out of it, the passion, the adventure have been replaced by shadows, and the host himself no longer there.

Is that the truth of it—the church as museum, as echo? Many would say so. In the part of the world where I come from, the people who say so are apt to be some of the wisest, most concerned people there are. They have little or nothing to do with the church because for them the church speaks a dead language, is for them a dead-end street. And if we are honest, you and I—we who are the church and try to hold on to whatever there is to hold on to in it—I think we have to admit that often they are right. Often, I'm afraid, the church is a place where preachers preach not out of their depths but out of their shallows, and who, when they try to show forth the great transforming truths of the faith that once set the world on its ear, speak not out of the experience of those truths in their own lives but speak instead like American tourists abroad who believe that if only they say the hallowed old words often enough and forcibly enough, everybody will be bound to understand whether they know the language or not. Often, I'm afraid, the church is a place where bread and wine and prayers and hymns and worship have little more significance than the secret rites of a Greek-letter fraternity. Sadder still, the church often seems to be a gathering of men and women who, whatever they find there, take so little of it out into the world with them that if one of them were to sit down at McDonald's and say grace, or say or do anything to suggest he or she is a Christian, the golden arches would shake with astonishment—and so, I suspect, would we. I think of an organization like Alcoholics Anonymous, which has no building, no budget, no priesthood, but only people who come together wherever they are to seek help in their helplessness from each other and from God and who are ready at any ungodly moment of day or night—which is to say, of course, at any godly moment—to go to each other's rescue, whereas you and I, who are called above all things to be Christs to each other, tend to pass like ships in the night. In our own genteel and unobtrusive ways will we "steal, murder, commit adultery, swear falsely, go after other gods, and then come before [him] into this house which is called by [his] name and say, 'We are delivered'?" The one who asks that question is Jeremiah, and there can be no great mystery as to whom he asks it of.

God is the Lord and giver of life. If the word *God* means anything that matters, something like that is what it means. Life-giver. Light-giver. God as giver of love that is both the peace that passes all understanding and a tiger in the blood, the one whom we hunger for even when all our words about God start to bore us to death. Is God in the Temple not just as a shadow, a word, but to give life to us where we are dead or dying, love to us where we are loveless and lost? Because if God is not to be found in the Temple, then maybe it is better that the Temple should be destroyed altogether so we can look for him where maybe he is to be found.

Each of us has an Exodus to remember. For each of us

a journey has begun. "We are delivered," we say, and yes, somewhere, somehow that is part of the truth of us. But we are also derelict. That is the other part. We have seen just enough of the day to know that it is night. "We do not see our signs; there is no longer any prophet," the Psalmist says. There is only that odd pair in that shabby restaurant. "And there is none among us who knows how long," the Psalmist says—night as the absence of God where we look for God to be present. But then the Psalmist speaks a word which of all his words to us is the most precious. "And yet," he says. And yet. "Thine is the day, thine also is the night."

"Behold the days are coming, says the Lord, when . . . I will put my law within them, and I will write it upon their hearts; and I will be their God, and they shall be my people." That is what Jeremiah said, who predicted the destruction of the Temple. "It is to your advantage that I go away, for if I do not go away, the Counselor will not come to you; but if I go, I will send him to you." That is what Jesus said, who predicted his own destruction.

There is nothing the world can't destroy if it puts its mind to it, including the world itself. The Temple of Solomon was destroyed as much by the Jews within as by the Babylonians without. And the church as the body of Christ is destroyed not just from without by a world that sees it as a dead-end street but by people like you and me who destroy it from within by our deadness and staleness, our failure to be brave, to be human, to take chances; by the sterility and irrelevance and superficiality and faddishness of so much of our churchly business and by our tragic-comic failure to move around in the world as though being a Christian makes not just a nominal difference but all the difference in the world. But if the Temple can be destroyed, and maybe deserves to be destroyed, God is not destroyed, Jeremiah says. Even if the Temple lies in ruins, God will find a new place to pitch his tent, and that place is the human heart: the law to be put within us, the Counselor to come, the breath of life.

Which hearts and where then? In whose hearts does something of God well up, something of new life start to live? I think of the Catholic bishops with their statements about nuclear disarmament. I think of the peace movement which it's easy enough to be critical about but which begins to make sisters and brothers even of enemies by trumpeting into the night that the achievement of no good we desire and the defeat of no evil we fear is worth the price of holocaust. I think of Alcoholics Anonymous, with their churchless church. And I think of that old woman and that small boy again, and of every old boy and small woman anywhere who for Christ's sake are willing to look like fools, who in some small and improbable way remind the rest of us of that simplicity and passion and outlandishness of faith without which no Temple, no church, is worth two cents, and to lose which, for you and me, is to lose our own souls.

Sisters and brothers, we must love one another or die. Surer than the law of gravity is sure, that is the law. And in those hearts where that law is written and kept, there the Counselor has come and God dwells, and the world itself begins to become the Temple. "O God, direct thy steps to the perpetual ruins" that can never ruin thee. Direct thy steps to us and to thy church in its emptiness and darkness. Thine is the day, but thine also is the night. Thine also is the night.

13. Delay

ISAIAH 9:2–7

The people who walked in darkness have seen a great light; those who dwell in a land of deep darkness, on them has light shined. Thou hast multiplied the nation, thou hast increased its joy; . . . For every boot of the tramping warrior in battle tumult and every garment rolled in blood will be burned as fuel for the fire. For to us a child is born, to us a son is given; and the government will be upon his shoulder, and his name will be called "Wonderful Counselor, Mighty God, Everlasting Father, Prince of Peace." Of the increase of his government and of peace there shall be no end, upon the throne of David, and over his kingdom, to establish it and to uphold it with justice and with righteousness, from this time forth and forevermore. The zeal of the Lord of hosts will do this.

JOHN 1:45–51

Philip found Nathanael, and said to him, "We have found him of whom Moses in the law and also the prophets wrote, Jesus of Nazareth, the son of Joseph." Nathanael said to him, "Can anything good come out of Nazareth?" Philip said to him, "Come and see." Jesus saw Nathanael coming to him, and said of him, "Behold, an Israelite indeed, in whom is no guile!" Nathanael said to him, "How do you know me?" Jesus answered him, "Before Philip called you, when you were under the fig tree, I saw you." Nathanael answered him, "Rabbi, you are the Son of God! You are the King of Israel!" Jesus answered him, "Because I said to you, I saw you under the fig tree, do you believe? You shall see greater things than these." And he said to him, "Truly, truly, I say to you, you will see heaven opened, and the angels of God ascending and descending upon the Son of man."

You have to take a long drive somewhere, say, and set out well before dawn to make a good start. It is winter, and the snow is coming down heavily. The headlights catch the tumbling flakes a little way ahead of you, but otherwise, all around you, there is nothing you can see. The darkness is so complete that it seems less an absence of light than itself a presence, a darkness so dense and impenetrable, like the snow itself, that what little light you have on your own can barely survive in it. It is hard to believe that it will ever be day again. There is no sky for the sun to rise in, and except for the short stretch of road that your car lights up, there is no earth; there is nothing to get your bearings by, nobody anywhere to point you on your way or reassure you by the sound of a human voice. As you travel slowly into the night, it's as if night travels slowly into you until the darkness without starts to become indistinguishable from the darkness within, darkness piling up in you like snow. It's as if it's not just someplace far away out there that you're moving toward but someplace even farther away in here, in you. Daybreak is what in every sense you're hoping toward, the coming of light into every kind of darkness. Light to see by—to see the road and whatever awaits at the road's end, to see another human being, to see yourself as human. It is winter. It is deep night. The snow muffles all sound except the faint hum of the engine, the ticking of the dashboard clock. Like an ancient pagan at the winter solstice, you feel there is maybe nothing too precious to sacrifice, nothing you would not be willing to give or do or be, if you only knew what, to make day come.

Or say instead that on just such another winter night it is not you who are journeying out but somebody who is journeying home to you. The roads are icy, and the radio has been full of accident reports. You've been waiting a long time. There comes a point where you can't bear just to sit there any longer; you go stand at the window to watch for the lights of cars. Every once in a while one appears out of the dark, and with your eyes, more than your eyes, you follow it up the long hill and around the bend, waiting to hear it slow down as it nears your house, waiting to see the little directional signal flicker a turn into your drive. But one after another, the cars all pass by and continue up the hill out of sight with stretches of silence in between them so long and empty that it's hard to believe in even the possibility of another car ever breaking that silence again—a silence too deep for any sound ever to well up out of it, a dark too thick for any light to pierce.

An hour late becomes an hour and a half, two hours late. You try to find something to take your mind off it— a book to read, the dishwasher to empty, a prayer to pray —but there's too much more of you involved by now than just your mind, and you can feel your face grow gray with waiting. Will the telephone ring like a fire alarm? Or will there be only more darkness, more silence? Or will your prayer finally be answered? So deep is your hoping that at moments hope itself drives back the night a little; and in your mind, if nowhere else, in the darkness of your waiting, what you hope to happen all but does happen. You all but see a light move slowly up the hill. You all but hear a car slow down as if to turn. Can it conceivably be? Silence fills your ears, darkness fills your eyes and more than your eyes. Is it only inside yourself that somewhere you hear a door opening? The sound of footsteps in the hall? From some distant part of the house, some deep and distant part of who you are, the one voice out of all the voices in the world you wait for calls out your name. Does it? Will it? Will the one you hope for ever come out of the hopelessness of such a night?

Or say, finally, that it is night, and you are home, and no one you love is in danger. You alone are in danger. The hospital has taken certain tests, say, and how they will turn out, only time will tell. Your life may just depend on how they turn out. So you lie there in the dark straining to hear time's tale ahead of time, because waiting time is always time strained, time searched and listened to, till past time, present time, future time all start to whisper at once—the past in all its preciousness and never more precious than now; the present in all its dark impenetrability; the future in whatever form it is to come. Morning will come at last, and with it the word you wait for will be spoken at last: the word that you hope for, long for, until you can all but hear it already, which is the word, of course, that gives you back your life again.

For light to come. For the one you love to come. For the word of life to be spoken. Faith is a way of waiting—never quite knowing, never quite hearing or seeing, because in the darkness we are all but a little lost. There is doubt hard on the heels of every belief, fear hard on the heels of every hope, and many holy things lie in ruins because the world has ruined them and we have ruined them. But faith waits even so, delivered at least from that final despair which gives up waiting altogether because it sees nothing left worth waiting for. Faith waits—for the opening of a door, the sound of footsteps in the hall, that beloved voice delayed, delayed, so long that there are times when you all but give up hope of ever hearing it.

And when at moments you think you do hear it (if only faintly, from far away) the question is: Can it possibly be, impossibly be, that one voice of all voices?

"Come and see," Philip says, says it to Nathanael, to all of us. "We have found him," Philip says. Found whom? Found what? "The one of whom Moses in the law and also the prophets wrote," Philip says. He means holiness itself, of course, giver of light and life, the beloved one whom all the world has been awaiting and will always await whether it knows it does or not. There are times when you can sense even the trees waiting, the stones, the dumb beasts. It's as if not just Nathanael, whoever he was, but all of us, whoever we are, hold our breath—history itself holds its breath—to hear who it is that Philip has found. Then Philip tells. "Jesus," he says, a name like any other name. "From Nazareth," he says, a place like any other place. Joseph's child.

The longing is so rich. Philip's words are so meager. "Jesus of Nazareth," he says. It seems hardly more than the brushing of snow against the windshield, the creak of the old house as you watch at the window, the beat of your own heart as you lie in bed waiting for morning. Do you laugh? Do you cry? Nathanael in a way does both with his half bitter, half sad little shrug of a joke. "Can anything good come out of Nazareth?" he asks. Can anything that matters so much come out of anywhere that seems to matter so little, let alone can something that matters more than anything else in the world because that is what Jesus is, Philip says. That is how Jesus matters. For thousands of years, since Moses' time, he is the one we've been waiting for, Philip says. The light that the darkness has been waiting for. Joseph's child. Out of no place, nowhere.

Nathanael's shrug is the shrug of us all if we're honest, I think. Can any one life shed light on the mystery of life itself? In some new and shattering way, can any one life make us come alive ourselves, because that is of course what we wait for, what religion is about—what churches are about, what our hymns and preaching and prayers are all about, though there are times you would hardly know it. *Life:* that's what we all hunger for, wait for always, whether we keep coming back to places like church to find it or whether we avoid places like church like the plague as the last places on earth to find it: both delivered in part and derelict in part, immigrants and mongrels all of us. It's life as we've never really known it but only dreamed it that we wait for. Life with each other. Life for each other. Life with the darkness gone. And they have found it, Philip says. They have found him. Can it be true?

The danger is that we'll say yes too easily, that we'll say it because all these centuries the church has been saying it and because for years we have been saying it ourselves. To say yes too easily, too much out of old habit, is to say it as if we really know who Jesus is, as if he is somehow *our* Jesus. He is not ours. If anything, we are his. He is Joseph's child. He is also Mystery's child. Who he is for our world, for us, we can know only from him. "Come and see," Philip says, and there is no other way for any of us. There was just a little way for Nathanael to travel—just around the bend in the road and across a patch of field—but in a sense Nathanael had been traveling there his whole life long as in a sense you and I have too: to see at last and to be seen, to know and to be known, to find and to be found.

There is a game we play sometimes. If we could somehow meet one of the great ones of history, which one would we choose? Would it be Shakespeare, maybe, because nobody knew better than he the Hamlet of us and the Ophelia of us, nobody knew better than he this midsummer night's dream of a darkly enchanted world. Or maybe it would be Abraham Lincoln, with feet no less of clay than our own feet, but whose face, in those last great photographs, seems somehow to have not only all of human suffering in it but traces of goodness and compassion that seem almost more than human. Or maybe it would be Saint Joan, the Maid of Orleans, whose very weakness was her strength, her innocence her armor, lighting up the dark skies of the fifteenth century like a star. But the great ones of the world, if you and I were to meet them, would have nothing to give us but their greatness, nothing to ask of us but our admiration; and we would go to such a meeting full of awe to be sure but knowing more or less what to expect. In the saints and heroes of the past, we would find someone greater than we are, more human, more complete, but cut from the same cloth as we are after all, someone who was as often lost, as full of doubt, as full of hope, waiting no less than you and I wait for we're not sure what to deliver us at last.

But if Philip is right, it is not just somebody greater than we whom we go to meet, and it is not just out of the past that he comes to meet us. It is not just his greatness that he has to give us. It is himself that he has to give us. It is ourselves that he has to give us. That is our faith. And it is not just our admiration that he asks. Who of us knows fully what he has to ask any more than we know fully what he has to give? And it is our not knowing that makes our meeting with him more momentous than any other we can imagine. It is the one whom Moses and the prophets foretold, Philip says. It is the Word made flesh. It is the word of all words that speaks out of deepest mystery to the flesh and blood of all of us.

Around the bend in the road and across the patch of field. Driving through the snowy night. Standing at the dark window. Lying in bed waiting for dawn to bring whatever word dawn brings. The one we await is the one whom for all these years we have prayed to, prayed through. We are Nathanael. Come and see, Philip tells us.

So we come as Nathanael came to see for ourselves if it is true what Philip says and what for all our lives we sometimes believed and sometimes failed to believe. We are men and women of the world, all of us are. We don't believe in fairy tales, at least not many of them, not often. Many of our best dreams have turned out to be only dreams. Many of our dearest hopes for ourselves and for the people we love have died stillborn, and the world has long since taught us to be prepared always for the worst. But we come nevertheless—come in faith. We make our way to where he stands beyond a little grove of trees, whoever we are—a retired schoolteacher half sick with boredom and loneliness, a young dancer at the peak of her career, an out-of-work black woman facing a mastectomy, a middle-aged couple trying to hold their marriage together, a boy and girl in love. And you and I come with them—like them, the bearers of secrets we have never told, the guardians of memories more precious than gold and sadder than an empty house. As we make our way through the trees, a figure comes into view. It is dusk, and he stands dark against the grey sky. At the sound of our footsteps, he glances our way. We stand for a moment with our eyes lowered, not daring to look up and see his face, for fear both of what it may be and of what it may fail to be. We have waited so long. We have traveled so far.

What Nathanael saw when he raised his eyes at last and looked up into that face we do not know, and we do not know either what you and I will see if such a moment should come also for us when we too shall stand before his justice and his love at last with all our secrets laid bare. But I believe that for us, as for Nathanael, it will be a face we recognize because at some level of our being it is a face that we have always known the way the birds of the air know from a distance of a thousand miles their place of nesting, the way the trees of the forest, even in winter, are rooted deep in the promise of spring. We will know him when we see him, and, more crucial still, he will know us.

"Behold, an Israelite indeed, in whom is no guile," Jesus says to Nathanael before Nathanael has found a tongue to say anything to him; and we picture this Nathanael standing there in all his guilenesses with mud on his shoes and his jaw hanging loose before he says finally, whispers it, I suspect, "Rabbi, you are the Son of God! You are the King of Israel!" And I picture you and me standing there too, not guileless by a long shot if you're anything like me, but full of all that the world has filled us with—and that we have filled the world with—in the way of disillusion and doubt and self-seeking and love and fear and deceit and hope and everything else that makes us, each in our own unrepeatable way, human.

Behold us for what we truly and helplessly are. Behold us each for what we have it in us to become and at our best moments pray to become and again and again choose not to become, can find no way of becoming. Behold every man and woman of us, everywhere, who spend most of our lives believing that we wait only for morning to break, for the beloved to return, for some word of comfort to be spoken. Behold all of us who, half-blinded by all that blinds us, find it hard to believe that we ourselves have been awaited ever since the creation of the world.

"The people who walked in darkness have seen a great light; those who dwelt in a land of deep darkness, on them has the light shined." Deep is the darkness of our time—of our land and of all lands and of all of us. And most of what light comes our way is as random and elusive as the lights of cars winding up the long hill at night. It is not a great light we have seen but only a small light. But we have come here anyway because somewhere, sometime, once, for all of us, an exodus happened, a grim sea parted, and we were delivered enough from bondage to ourselves to see at least where true deliverance lies. We have come here because although there is always much in the world and much in ourselves that drives us toward despair, and although we ourselves are often among those who lay waste the Temple in its holiness, we have never been abandoned in our dereliction by the one whom no Temple can ever contain. And the great light that our small light foretells is that the one who from the beginning has led us out, led us forth, and who has been with us through the perpetual ruins we have wandered in ever since, and through the long delay, is the one whom we wait for in great hope and who in great hope waits also for us. Listen to your lives for the sound of him. Search even in the dark for the light and the love and the life because they are there also, and we are known each one by name.

And the name of the one who waits for us? It is Wonderful Counselor, Mighty God. It is Everlasting Father, Mother, Princess and Prince of Peace. "And you shall see greater things than this" are the words that come to us as they came to Nathanael before us. Much that we hold fast to we will have to let loose, and much that we have lost we will have to find again; and for those as long accustomed to the dark as we, the great light will doubtless bring great tribulation as well as great benediction before we rise up in the splendor of it whole and new at last. But greater things than this we shall see is the promise, and, by God's grace, greater things than this we shall become.

"Truly, truly, I say to you, you will see heaven opened, and the angels of God ascending and descending upon the Son of man" and upon us all. May we never deceive ourselves that we know what those words mean. If we think they are no more than the florid poetry of another age we only reveal how captive we are to the narrow presuppositions of our own. If we think they are to be taken as literally as a child would take them, I suspect we are more nearly right but only clumsily, partially, in the manner of children. Who can know fully what Christ means when he says that we will see him in his glory? But because we have already seen him in the glory of our long delayed but dearest hope, I believe that the faith is by no means blind that sees his word as not just a poem, and only a poem, but as high and unimaginable truth. Amen. Come, Lord Jesus.

14. The Road Goes On

JOHN 14:6
Jesus said to him, "I am the way, and the truth, and the life."

Here I am, and there you are. That is the crux of it. Here
I am, the stranger in your midst. There you are, who are
the midst, who are the graduating class, who are friends
and classmates and sweethearts of each other, who have
brought your friends and families with you and yet who
are—all of you, even those of you who have known each
other for years and whose hearts are sweetest—as much
strangers to each other in many ways as I am a stranger to
you all. Because how can we be other than strangers when
at those rare moments of our lives when we stop hiding
from each other and try instead passionately and profoundly to make ourselves known to each other, we find
this is precisely what we cannot do?

And yet in another sense we are none of us strangers.
Not even I. Not even you. Because how can we be strangers when, for all these years, we have ridden on the
back of this same rogue planet, when we have awakened
to the same sun and dreamed the same dreams under the
same moon? How can we be strangers when we are all
of us in the same interior war and do battle with the

same interior enemy, which is most of the time ourselves? How can we be strangers when we laugh and cry
at the same things and have the same bad habits and occasionally astonish ourselves and everybody else by per-
forming the same uncharacteristic deeds of disinterested
kindness and love?

We are strangers and we are not strangers. The question is: Can anything that really matters humanly pass between us? The question is: Can God in his grace and
power speak anything that matters ultimately through the
likes of me to the likes of you? And I am saying all these
things not just to point up the difficulties of delivering a
commencement address like this. Who cares about that? I
am saying them because in the place where I am standing
now, or places just as improbable, you will be standing
soon enough as your turn comes. And much of what this
day means is that your turn has come at last.

As ministers, preachers, prophets, pastors, teachers,
administrators and who knows what-all else of churches,
you will be leaving this lovely place for places as lovely or
lovelier yet or not lovely at all where you will take your
turn at doing essentially what I am here to do now, which
is one way or another to be, however inadequately, a
servant of Christ. I wouldn't have dreamed of packing my
bag and driving a thousand miles except for Christ. I
wouldn't have the brass to stand here before you now if
the only words I had to speak were the ones I had cooked
up for the occasion. I am here, Heaven help me, because
I believe that from time to time we are given something
of Christ's word to speak if we can only get it out through
the clutter and cleverness of our own speaking. And I
believe that in the last analysis, whatever other reasons

you have for being here yourselves, Christ is at the bottom of why you are here too. We are all here because of him. This is his day as much as, if not more than, it is ours. If it weren't for him, we would be somewhere else.

Our business is to be the hands and feet and mouths of one who has no other hands or feet or mouth except our own. It gives you pause. Our business is to work for Christ as surely as men and women in other trades work for presidents of banks or managers of stores or principals of high schools. Whatever salaries you draw, whatever fringe benefits you receive, your recompense will be ultimately from Christ, and a strange and unforeseeable and wondrous recompense I suspect it will be, and with many a string attached to it too. Whatever real success you have will be measured finally in terms of how well you please not anyone else in all this world—including your presbyteries, your bishops, your congregations—but only Christ, and I suspect that the successes that please him best are very often the ones that we don't even notice. Christ is the one who will be hurt, finally, by your failures. If you are to be healed, comforted, sustained during the dark times that will come to you as surely as they have come to everyone else who has ever gone into this strange trade, Christ will be the one to sustain you because there is no one else in all this world with love enough and power enough to do so. It is worth thinking about.

Christ is our employer as surely as the general contractor is the carpenter's employer, only the chances are that this side of Paradise we will never see his face except mirrored darkly in dreams and shadows, if we're lucky, and in each other's faces. He is our general, but the chances are that this side of Paradise we will never hear his voice except in the depth of our own inner silence and in each other's voices. He is our shepherd, but the chances are we will never feel his touch except as we are touched by the joy and pain and holiness of our own life and each other's lives. He is our pilot, our guide, our true, fast, final friend and judge, but often when we need him most, he seems farthest away because he will always have gone on ahead, leaving only the faint print of his feet on the path to follow. And the world blows leaves across the path. And branches fall. And darkness falls. We are, all of us, Mary Magdalene, who reached out to him at the end only to embrace the empty air. We are the ones who stopped for a bite to eat that evening at Emmaus and, as soon as they saw who it was that was sitting there at the table with them, found him vanished from their sight. Abraham, Moses, Gideon, Rahab, Sarah are our brothers and sisters because, like them, we all must live *in faith,* as the great chapter puts it with a staggering honesty that should be a lesson to us all, "not having received what was promised, but having seen it and greeted it from afar," and only from afar. And yet the country we seek and do not truly find, at least not here, not now, the heavenly country and homeland, is there somewhere as surely as our yearning for it is there; and I think that our yearning for it is itself as much a part of the truth of it as our yearning for love or beauty or peace is a part of those truths. And Christ is there with us on our way as surely as the way itself is there that has brought us to this place. It has brought us. We are here. He is with us—that is our faith—but only in unseen ways, as subtle and pervasive as air. As for what it remains for you and me to do, maybe T. S. Eliot says it as poignantly as anybody.

. . .wait without hope
For hope would be hope of the wrong thing; wait without
    love
For love would be love of the wrong thing; there is yet
    faith
But the faith and the love and the hope are all in the
    waiting.
Wait without thought, for you are not ready for thought:
So the darkness shall be light, and the stillness the dancing.

It's a queer business that you have chosen or that has chosen you. It's a business that breaks the heart for the sake of the heart. It's a hard and chancy business whose risks are as great even as its rewards. Above all else, perhaps, it is a crazy business. It is a foolish business. It is a crazy and foolish business to work for Christ in a world where most people most of the time don't give a hoot in hell whether you work for him or not. It is crazy and foolish to offer a service that most people most of the time think they need like a hole in the head. As long as there are bones to set and drains to unclog and children to tame and boredom to survive, we need doctors and plumbers and teachers and people who play the musical saw; but when it comes to the business of Christ and his church, how unreal and irrelevant a service that seems even, and at times especially, to the ones who are called to work at it.

"We are fools for Christ's sake," Paul says. You can't put it much more plainly than that. God is foolish too, he says—"the foolishness of God"—just as plainly. God is foolish to choose for his holy work in the world the kind of lamebrains and misfits and nitpickers and holier-than-thous and stuffed shirts and odd ducks and egomaniacs and milquetoasts and closet sensualists as are vividly repre-

sented here by you and me this spring evening. God is
foolish to send us out to speak hope to a world that slogs
along heart-deep in the conviction that from here on out
things can only get worse. To speak of realities we cannot
see when the realities we see all too well are already more
than we can handle. To speak of loving our enemies when
we have a hard enough time of it just loving our friends.
To be all things to all people when it's usually all we can
do to be anything that matters much to anybody. To proclaim eternal life in a world that is as obsessed with death
as a quick browse through *TV Guide* or the newspapers or
the drugstore paperbacks make plain enough. God is foolish to send us out on a journey for which there are no sure
maps. Such is the foolishness of God.

And yet. The "and yet" of it is our faith, of course.
And yet, Paul says, "the foolishness of God is wiser than
men," which is to say that in some unsearchable way he
may even know what he is doing. Praise him.

If I were braver than I am, I would sing you a song at
this point. If you were braver than you are, you might
even encourage me to. But let me at least say you a song.
It is from *The Lord of the Rings,* and Bilbo Baggins sings it.
It goes like this.

> The road goes ever on and on
> Down from the door where it began.
> Now far ahead the road has gone,
> And I must follow if I can,
> Pursuing it with weary feet,
> Until it joins some larger way,
> Where many paths and errands meet.
> And whither then?
> I cannot say.

"I am the way," Jesus said. I am the road. And in some foolish fashion, we are all on the road that is his, that is he, or such at least is our hope and prayer. That is why we are here at this turning of the road. There is not a single shoe in this place that does not contain a foot of clay, a foot that drags, a foot that stumbles; but on just such feet we all seek to follow that road through a world where there are many other roads to follow, and hardly a one of them that is not more clearly marked and easier to tramp and toward an end more known, more assured, more realizable. But we have picked this road, or been picked by it. "I am the way," he said, "the truth and the life." We have come this far along the *way*. From time to time, when we have our wits about us, when our hearts are in the right place, when nothing more enticing or immediate shows up to distract us, we have glimpsed that *truth*. From time to time when the complex and wearisome and seductive business of living doesn't get in our way, our pulses have quickened and gladdened to the pulse of that *life*. Who knows what the mysteries of our faith mean? Who knows what the Holy Spirit means? Who knows what the Resurrection means? Who knows what he means when he tells us that whenever two or three are gathered together in his name, he will be with them? But what at the very least they seem to mean is that there winds through all we think of as real life a way of life, a way to life, that is so vastly realer still that we cannot think of him, whose way it is, as anything less than vastly alive.

By grace we are on that way. By grace there come unbidden moments when we feel in our bones what it is like to be on that way. Our clay feet drag us to the bedroom of the garrulous old woman, to the alcoholic who for the tenth time has phoned to threaten suicide just as we are sitting down to supper, to the laying of the cornerstone of the new gym to deliver ourselves of a prayer that nobody much listens to, to the Bible study group where nobody has done any studying, to the Xerox machine. We don't want to go. We go in fear of the terrible needs of the ones we go to. We go in fear of our own emptiness from which it is hard to believe that any word or deed of help or hope or healing can come. But we go because it is where his way leads us; and again and again we are blessed by our going in ways we can never anticipate, and our going becomes a blessing to the ones we go to because when we follow his way, we never go entirely alone, and it is always something more than just ourselves and our own emptiness that we bring. Is that true? Is it true in the sense that it is true that there are seven days in a week and that light travels faster than sound? Maybe the final answer that faith can give to that awesome and final question occurs in a letter that Dostoevski wrote to a friend in 1854. "If anyone proved to me that Christ was outside the truth," he wrote, "and it really was so that the truth was outside Christ, then I would prefer to remain with Christ than with the truth."

"The road goes ever on and on," the song says, "down from the door where it began," and for each of us there was a different door, and we all have different tales to tell of where and when and how our journeys began. Perhaps there was no single moment but rather a series of moments that together started us off. For me, there was hearing a drunken blasphemy in a bar. There was a dream where I found myself writing down a name which, though I couldn't remember it when I woke up, I knew was the true and secret name of everything that matters or could ever matter. As I lay on the grass one afternoon thinking that if ever I was going to know the truth in all its fullness, it was going to be then, there was a stirring in the air that made two apple branches strike against each other with a wooden clack, and I suspect that any more of the truth than that would have been the end of me instead of, as it turned out, part of the beginning.

Such moments as those, and others no less foolish, were, together, the door from which the road began for me, and who knows where it began for each of you. But this much at least, I think, would be true for us all: that one way or another the road starts off from passion—a passion for what is holy and hidden, a passion for Christ. It is a little like falling in love, or, to put it more accurately, I suppose, falling in love is a little like it. The breath quickens. Scales fall from the eyes. A world within the world flames up. If you are Simeon Stylites, you spend the rest of your days perched on a flagpole. If you are Saint Francis, you go out and preach to the red-winged blackbirds. If you are Albert Schweitzer, you give up theology and Bach and go to medical school. And if that sort of thing is too rich for your blood, you go to a seminary. You did. I did. And for some of us, it's not all that crazy a thing to do.

It's not such a crazy thing to do because if seminaries don't as a rule turn out saints and heroes, they at least teach you a thing or two. "God has made foolish the wisdom of the world," Paul says, but not until wisdom has served its purpose. Passion is all very well. It is all very well to fall in love. But passion must be grounded, or like lightning without a lightning rod it can blow fuses and burn the house down. Passion must be related not just to the world inside your skin where it is born but to the world outside your skin where it has to learn to walk and talk and act in terms of social justice and human need and politics and nuclear power and God knows what-all else or otherwise become as shadowy and irrelevant as all the other good intentions that the way to hell is paved with. Passion must be harnessed and put to work, and the power that first stirs the heart must become the power that also stirs the hands and feet because it is the places your feet take you to and the work you find for your hands that finally proclaim who you are and who Christ is. Passion without wisdom to give it shape and direction is as empty as wisdom without passion to give it power and purpose. So you sit at the feet of the wise and learn what they have to teach, and our debts to them are so great that, if your experience is like mine, even twenty-five years later you will draw on the depth and breadth of their insights, and their voices will speak in you still, and again and again you will find yourself speaking in their voices. You learn as much as you can from the wise until finally, if you do it right and things break your way, you are wise enough to be yourself, and brave enough to speak with your own voice, and foolish enough, for Christ's sake, to live and serve out of the uniqueness of your own vision of him and out of your own passion.

"And whither then?" the song asks. The world of *The Lord of the Rings* is an enchanted world. It is a shadowy world where life and death are at stake and where things are seldom what they seem. It is a dangerous and beautiful world in which great evil and great good are engaged in a battle where more often than not the odds are heavily

in favor of great evil. It is a world where enormous bur-
dens are loaded on small shoulders and where the most
fateful issues hang on what are apparently the most
homely and insignificant decisions. And thus it is through
a world in many ways much like our own that the road
winds.

You will be ordained, many of you, or have been
already, and if again your experience is anything like
mine, you will find, or have found, that something more
even than an outlandish new title and an outlandish new
set of responsibilities is conferred in that outlandish cere-
mony. Without wanting to sound unduly fanciful, I think
it is fair to say that an extraordinary new adventure begins
with ordination, a new stretch of the road, that is unlike
any other that you have either experienced or imagined.
Your life is no longer your own in the same sense. You
are not any more virtuous than you ever were—certainly
no new sanctity or wisdom or power suddenly descends—
but you are nonetheless "on call" in a new way. You start
moving through the world as the declared representative
of what people variously see as either the world's oldest
and most persistent and superannuated superstition, or the
world's wildest and most improbable dream, or the holy,
living truth itself. In unexpected ways and at unexpected
times people of all sorts, believers and unbelievers alike,
make their way to you looking for something that often
they themselves can't name any more than you can well
name it to them. Often their lives touch yours at the moments when they are most vulnerable, when some great
grief or gladness or perplexity has swept away all the usual
barriers we erect between each other so that you see them
for a little as who they really are, and you yourself are
stripped naked by their nakedness.

Strange things happen. Again and again Christ is present not where, as priests, you would be apt to look for him but precisely where you wouldn't have thought to look for him in a thousand years. The great preacher, the sunset, the Mozart Requiem can leave you cold, but the child in the doorway, the rain on the roof, the half-remembered dream, can speak of him and for him with an eloquence that turns your knees to water. The decisions you think are most important turn out not to matter so much after all, but whether or not you mail the letter, the way you say goodbye or decide not to say it, the afternoon you cancel everything and drive out to the beach to watch the tide come in—these are apt to be the moments when souls are won or lost, including quite possibly your own.

You come to places where many paths and errands meet, as the song says, as all our paths meet for a moment here, we friends who are strangers, we strangers who are friends. Great possibilities for good or for ill may come of the meeting, and often it is the leaden casket rather than the golden casket that contains the treasure, and the one who seems to have least to offer turns out to be the one who has most.

"And whither then?" Whither now? "I cannot say," the singer says, nor yet can I. But far ahead the road goes on anyway, and we must follow if we can because it is our road, it is his road, it is the only road that matters when you come right down to it. Let me finally say only this one thing more.

I was sitting by the side of the road one day last fall. It was a dark time in my life. I was full of anxiety, full of fear and uncertainty. The world within seemed as shadowy as the world without. And then, as I sat there, I spotted a car coming down the road toward me with one of those license plates that you can get by paying a little extra with a word on it instead of just numbers and a letter or two. And of all the words the license plate might have had on it, the word that it did have was the word T-R-U-S-T: TRUST. And as it came close enough for me to read, it became suddenly for me a word from on high, and I give it to you here as a word from on high also for you, a kind of graduation present.

The world is full of dark shadows to be sure, both the world without and the world within, and the road we've all set off on is long and hard and often hard to find, but the word is *trust*. Trust the deepest intuitions of your own heart. Trust the source of your own truest gladness. Trust the road. Above all else, trust him. Trust him. Amen.

15. Summons to Pilgrimage

At its heart, religion is mysticism. Moses with his flocks in Midian, Buddha under the Bo tree, Jesus up to his knees in the waters of Jordan: each of them responds to Something for which words like shalom, oneness, God even, are only pallid souvenirs. "I have seen things," Aquinas told a friend, "that make all my writings seem like straw." Religion as institution, ethics, dogma, ritual, scripture, social action—all of this comes later and in the long run maybe counts for less. Religions start, as Frost said poems do, with a lump in the throat, to put it mildly, or with the bush going up in flames, the rain of flowers, the dove coming down out of the sky.

As for the man in the street, wherever his own religion is a matter of more than custom it is apt to be because, however dimly, a doorway opened in the air once to him too, a word was spoken, and, however shakily, he too responded. The debris of his life continues to accumulate, the Vesuvius of the years scatters its ashes deep and much gets buried alive, but even under many layers the telltale heart can go on beating still.

Where it beats strong, there starts pulsing out from it

a kind of life that is marked by, above all things perhaps, compassion—that sometimes fatal capacity for feeling what it is like to live inside another's skin, knowing that there can never really be peace and joy for any until there is peace and joy finally for all. Where it stops beating altogether, little is left religiously speaking but a good man, not perhaps in Mark Twain's "worst sense of the word," but surely in the grayest and saddest: the good man whose goodness has become cheerless and finicky, a technique for working off his own guilts, a gift with no love in it which neither deceives nor benefits any for long.

Religion as a word points to that area of human experience where in one way or another man comes upon mystery as a summons to pilgrimage; where he senses meanings no less overwhelming because they can be only hinted at in myth and ritual; where he glimpses a destination that he can never know fully until he reaches it.

We are all of us more mystics than we believe or choose to believe—life is complicated enough as it is, after all. We have seen more than we let on, even to ourselves. Through some moment of beauty or pain, some sudden turning of our lives, we catch glimmers at least of what the saints are blinded by; only then, unlike the saints, we tend to go on as though nothing has happened. To go on as though something has happened, even though we are not sure what it was or just where we are supposed to go with it, is to enter the dimension of life that religion is a word for.

Some, of course, go to the typewriter. First the lump in the throat, the stranger's face unfurling like a flower, and then the clatter of the keys, the ting-a-ling of the right-hand margin. One thinks of Pascal sewing into his jacket, where after his death a servant found it, his "since about half past ten in the evening until about half past midnight. Fire. Certitude. Certitude. Feeling. Joy. Peace," stammering it out like a child because he had to. Fire, fire, and then the scratch of pen on paper. There are always some who have to set it down in black and white.

There are poetry books and there are poetic books—the first a book with poems in it, the second a book which may or may not have poems in it but which is in some sense itself a poem—and possibly a similar distinction can be made between religion books and religious books. A religion book is a book with religion in it in the everyday sense of religious ideas, symbols, attitudes, and, if it takes the form of fiction or drama, with characters and setting that to one degree or another have religious associations or implications.

In the field of fiction, there would be *The Scarlet Letter, Billy Budd,* Mann's Joseph tetralogy, Faulkner's *A Fable,* Hesse's *Siddhartha,* much of Graham Greene, much of Mauriac, and so on. And of course the element of religion need not dominate as in those but can be just one of many other things that are going on.

Christ symbols are to be found almost anywhere: Hemingway taking his Old Man up Calvary with his mast on his shoulder and his palms lacerated by fishline, the Beatles singing of the Fool on the Hill as "the man of a thousand voices" whom "nobody ever hears."

Characters also talk about religion in novels: old Mr. Hook in John Updike's *The Poorhouse Fair* fumbling through his arguments for the existence of God while the young Prefect, Conner, demolishes them one by one until in the process he is himself somehow demolished; Tarrou in *The Plague* asking the question which has in different forms come to preoccupy so many: "Can one be a saint without God?" Explicitly or implicitly, sometimes profoundly, sometimes superficially, a religion book tells us something about religion as a poetry book presents us with poems.

With religious books, we need more than our wits about us, maybe sometimes less. A religious book may or may not have religion in it, but what it does have is a certain openness to Mystery itself, and what it asks of us is also a certain openness, a certain suspension of either belief or disbelief. If we let it, the reading of a religious book can become in itself an experience of what, at its best, a religion book can only tell about. A religion book is a canvas, a religious book a transparency. With a religious book it is less what we see in it than what we see through it that matters.

J. R. R. Tolkien's fairy-tale epic *The Lord of the Rings* helps draw the distinction perhaps. Some of its admirers have tried to make it into a religion book by claiming, among other things, that the Ring of Power which must be destroyed is the hydrogen bomb. Tolkien, on the other hand, denied this unequivocally. But intended or otherwise, there can be little doubt that for many it has become a religious book. The "Frodo Lives" buttons are not entirely a joke, because something at least comes to life through those fifteen hundred pages, although inevitably it is hard to say just what.

It seems to have something to do with the way Tolkien has of making us see the quiddity of things like wood, bread, stone, milk, iron, as though we have never seen them before or not for a long time, which is probably the truth of the matter; his landscapes set deeper echoes going in us than any message could. He gives us back a sense that we have mostly lost of the things of the earth, and because we are ourselves of the earth, whatever else, we are given back too some sense of our own secret. Very possibly again he did not intend it. It may well be axiomatic that, religiously, a writer achieves most when he is least conscious of doing so. Certainly the attempt to be religious is as doomed as the attempt to be poetic is.

The word, I suppose, is *revelation*. Religious books always seem to end up being about ourselves in the sense not simply of illuminating our own experience but of opening up vistas into worlds that, until they were revealed to us, we never knew were home.

There is very little religion in Shakespeare, but when he is greatest, he is most religious. It is curious that the plays that fit this best are, like *The Lord of the Rings,* in their own way fairy tales. There is *The Tempest,* that masque of his old age where all comes right in the end, where like Rembrandt in his last self-portraits Shakespeare smiles up out of his wrinkles and speaks into the night a golden word too absurd to be anything perhaps but true, the laughter of things beyond the tears of things.

And there is *King Lear,* its Cinderella opening with the wicked sisters and the good one. But then the fairy tale is turned on its head, and although everything comes right in the end, everything also does not come right—religion books are usually tidier. Blinded, old Gloucester sees the truth about his sons but too late to save the day. Cordelia is vindicated in her innocence only to be destroyed more grotesquely because more pointlessly than her sisters in their lustful cunning. And Lear himself emerges from his madness to become truly a king at last, but dies then babbling that his dead darling lives and fumbling with a button at his throat.

Maybe fairy tales tend to become religious because if we read them at all, we have our guards up less. We are prepared for mystery. *The Brothers Karamazov,* a religious book par excellence, is among other things a murder mystery, and in murder mysteries too we are ready for the unexpected—ready to believe that it was the butler after all who did it, and when Alyosha kisses the earth and begs its forgiveness, ready to glimpse in ourselves and beyond an abyss of pity and longing deeper than we ever dreamed.

Finally a word about Graham Greene. To list *The End of the Affair* and *The Heart of the Matter* as religion books seems just. They are on the border, perhaps, between the religion book and the religious. But when it comes to *The Power and the Glory,* he seems to cross that border. The art is the same, there is the same concern with the subterranean presence of a grace that can save a man's soul even through his sin, and yet something else is here that is better heard than described.

Trying to escape north out of revolutionary Mexico, the whiskey-priest reaches a peasant village where he meets his bastard daughter for what turns out to be the last time. She is an ancient, malicious dwarf of a child who recoils, sniggering, when he first tries to embrace her. Greene writes:

> He said: "I love you. I am your father and I love you. Try to understand that." He held her tightly by the wrist and suddenly she stayed still, looking up at him. He said: "I would give my life, that's nothing, my soul . . . my dear, my

dear, try to understand that you are—so important." . . . She stared back at him out of dark and unconscious eyes: he had a sense that he had come too late. He said: "Good-bye, my dear," and clumsily kissed her—a silly infatuated aging man, who as soon as he released her and started padding back to the plaza could feel behind his hunched shoulders the whole vile world coming round the child to ruin her. His mule was there, saddled, by the gaseosa stall. A man said: "Better go north, father," and stood waving his hand. One mustn't have human affections—or rather one must love every soul as if it were one's own child. The passion to protect must extend itself over a world—but he felt it tethered and aching like a hobbled animal to the tree trunk. He turned the mule south.*

It is like Alice's looking-glass, I suppose, where we see at first our own homeliness—more than half in love, all of us, with our own sin, silly and doomed as we pad along disheveled ways—and then at last the glass melts away like a mist and opens out, for a moment at least, into looking-glass land. Nothing stays put there for long, and nothing is entirely what it seems. Victory and defeat, love and justice, sin and grace, life and death even—distinctions go dim and contrariwise. Beasts talk and flowers come alive. Both in the reading and in the writing, a religious book is an act of grace—no less rare, no less precious, no less wildly improbable.

---

*Graham Greene, *The Power and the Glory* (New York: The Viking Press, 1959), pp. 111–112.

16. God and Old Scratch

The Ouija board next to the Scrabble set. A voodoo gri-gri bristling pins like a porcupine between Barbi and Ken. Simon Magus, Cagliostro and Madame Blavatsky sharing honors with Archie Bunker, Snoopy and Joe Namath. The unpleasantness in seventeenth-century Salem more familiar than the twentieth-century shenanigans of Joe McCarthy. Horoscopes and kaleidoscopes. Tarot decks and Old Maid decks. Doctor Faustus and Doctor Seuss. Dracula and Disneyland. Telepathy and Terrytoons. It is no secret that in the world of the teenybopper, Rosemary's baby and Sybil Leek are giving the likes of Huck Finn, Holden Caulfield and the Hobbits of Middle Earth a run for their money. And it is no wonder either.

The spate of books for the young on the occult in general and witchcraft in particular is spine-chilling. ESP and astrology, ghosts and ghouls, magic and mesmerism, techniques of divination as old-hat as palmistry and as esoteric as alphitomancy (you do it with barley loaves) or belomancy (you do it with arrows)—they come in paperbacks and hardbacks, some dry and informative, some blood-soaked and hair-raising, and publishers' lists read like an incantation: *The Satanic Mill, The Compleat Werewolf, Masters of the Occult, The Modern Witch's Spellbook, Test Your ESP, The Visionary Girls, Ladies of Horror, The Active-Enzyme Lemon-Freshened Junior High School Witch, In Search of Ghosts,* to name just a few at random. Writers of fiction and nonfiction both, they know a bad thing when they see it, and everybody is getting into the act.

Is it a bad thing—literarily, psychologically, humanly? Who knows? It seems at least an understandable thing. Even without using arrows or barley loaves, one might almost have predicted it. It is on stormy nights that witches dance and ghosts gibber. Violence in the streets; racial disorder; an imperiled environment; scandals in high places; Black September; the specter always of thermonuclear holocaust: the children were bound to get wind of it eventually and to respond more or less like everybody else. The world is among other things so vast, dark, and disheveled that whether you are sixteen or sixty the temptation is always to turn from it to what is small, bright, and tidy—the stars, for instance. Sagittarius, Capricorn, Aquarius follow one another in stately syntax and make a kind of sense of things. They don't make it any easier to live with fools and knaves but at least they purport to explain why they are as they are. They don't make you master of your destiny, but at least they give utterance to what it is going to be, and forewarned is forearmed. Avoid trips by water on Tuesday, and on Wednesday expect a letter that may change your life. Populations may explode and strangers arrive from outer space, but there are always seventy-eight cards in the Tarot deck and sixty-four hexagrams in the *I Ching,* and whether or not they are actually infallible, at least they tend to look it more than most people do these days. Even Roger Mudd admits to being occasionally puzzled, and though the President seems to have it all down pat, the social science teacher has his doubts about the President.

When modern science can get man to the moon but not food to the starving; when the "best and brightest" can raise our highest hopes but, snarled in their own rhetoric, plunge us into our most abysmal war; when the combined efforts of religionists and humanitarians can prick our consciences and fill our stadiums but leave the human heart to all appearances as unregenerate as ever, it is time perhaps to consider turning from reason to Rhadamanthus, from Methodism to magic, from television to telepathy. If the living can't give us the answers, maybe the dead can. If we are helpless to move the powers that be, maybe by learning the right spell we can manipulate powers that even the powers that be must bow to. If God seems vague and far away, Old Scratch and his merry men seem more real and active than ever, and if we can't beat them, we can always join them. Besides which, whereas theology has never been much good at explaining the perennial presence and popularity of evil, demonology makes a specialty of it. Religion is complex and God unpredictable, but magic is comparatively simple, and with a lock of a pretty girl's hair and the right philtre you can make her yours every time.

In Ingmar Bergman's *The Seventh Seal,* the Knight tells the young witch being bound to the stake that he wants to meet the Devil, and when she asks him why, he says, "I want to ask him about God. He, if anyone, must know." Maybe that is part of it too. Maybe this generation of children turns to Gilles de Rais and Count Dracula partly

at least from the same impulse that led an earlier generation to turn to the lives of the saints and heroes: more than
most people, the young are curious about God, have a
hunch perhaps that in their own way maybe his enemies
have as much to tell about him as his friends and that his
absence in a human life may be as eloquent as his presence.

Or maybe this is all to take the current craze too seriously, or at least to forget that there are other ways of
taking it. Without question, part of why a child turns to
stories of hexing and haunting is simply that they are fun,
and fun because they are scary, and scary in a way that
everyday horrors are no longer apt to be because he has
seen so much of them on the flickering blue screen. Assas-
sinations, riots, the grieving of widows, the napalming of
children plus all the soap-opera disasters of crime and
death, drugs and divorce—they can still make a child's
heart beat faster and follow him into his dreams, but scare
him? Not so much anymore, the chances are. They are as
familiar as furniture and as remote as history, part of a
world he doesn't fully belong to, at least not yet awhile.
But the world of the supernatural is a world at his elbow.
It is a world no farther from him than the nearest darkened
stair or empty room, a world he enters, or that enters him,
every time the lights go out or the old house creaks, and
thus it is a world that has the power still to make the blood
run cold. Who can resist it? Being scared is fun in itself,
and when what you are scared by is an externalization *out
there* on the printed page of something even scarier *in here*
where your bad dreams come from, there is perhaps a kind
of therapy in it too. To be able to cope with the ghosts
without is a step on the way to being able to cope with the
ghosts within.

The world of the supernatural is also a world without rhyme, reason, or rules, and what child can resist that either? Parents, teachers, cops, draft boards, not all their superior know-how is worth any more than a rabbit's foot when it comes to dealing with a haunted house, and a witch can turn even a high-school principal into a pumpkin. It is a world too where the whole panoply of modern technology is refreshingly helpless. You can't detect a ghost with radar or remove a curse neurosurgically. The world of the supernatural is shadowy, will not compute, and that is much of its appeal. In a macadamized, shopping-center, IBM civilization, it is one of the few wilderness areas left.

Another one, of course, is the world of the fairy tale, and the differences between them are marked. In stories of the supernatural, outlines are blurred and normal distinctions tend to disappear. A ghost is neither alive nor dead. The message that comes through the Ouija board seems to make sense until suddenly it goes haywire and turns into nonsense. Dr. Jekyll is Dr. Jekyll, but he is also Mr. Hyde. Maybe Peter Quint really appears to the children, or maybe it is just in their minds. Good and evil, true and false, shadow and substance—they mingle and change shape before your eyes like ectoplasm. In fairy tales, just the opposite is true. There, the outlines are if anything sharper than in real life. Heroes are heroes and villains villains. Nobody mistakes the prince for a frog for long, and even when the wicked witch disguises herself as a beautiful maiden, underneath she is just as wicked as she always was. If the realm of the occult is the realm of the subconscious and the less-than-human where disorder prevails, the realm of faery is the realm of the imagination and the more-than-human where what prevails is not, to be sure, the earthbound order of men but the airy order of the immortals whereby, though flowers may talk and lobsters quadrille, purposes are inexorably worked out that are both darker and brighter than most we are familiar with this side of the moon. In fairy tales not everybody always lives happily ever after—the Steadfast Tin Soldier comes to a fiery end, and even once the ring of evil is destroyed, Frodo knows that the triumph of good is far from assured—but no matter how dark the things that happen, the implication of fairy tales is that darkness is not the ultimate reality, and thus, as Tolkien writes, they can give us "a catch of the breath, a beat and lifting of the heart, near to (or indeed accompanied by) tears, as keen as that given by any form of literary art." On the other hand, tales of the occult at their best can give us no more, if no less, than a creeping of the flesh, a chill shudder along the spine.

It is comforting, therefore, to know that both genres apparently thrive among the young. The Wizard of Oz, the Red Queen, the Psammead, Merlin, Aslan, are all in there still, together with the vampires, werewolves, warlocks and poltergeists. Maybe a child, or anyone else for that matter, does well to turn to both camps. The one reminds us of the chaotic, the chthonic, the primitive, which, from within if not from without, threaten always to overwhelm us. The other speaks to us of curious promises which, for all our sad skepticism, may even once above a time be kept; of good dreams which, whether they come true or not, help make bearable the night.

17. The Speaking and Writing of Words

Let me start with an experience we all have in common, the experience of taking a trip somewhere to see the sights. You get hold of a car and head off for the coast, say, or some famous old house, or some city you have never been to before. There are plenty of sights to see—the waves washing up over the flat sand, the Aeolian harp in the window at Emerson's house in Concord, the faces of strangers coming at you down the busy pavement like autumn leaves in the wind. And in addition to the sights you see there are also, of course, all the memories and thoughts and feelings those sights conjure up in you as you see them—the sense of beauty or peace or sadness, maybe, sometimes a sense of the past as both irrecoverable and yet somehow also almost uncannily present as though, if you just knew how to do it, you could fold back the air like a curtain and see it all going on still before your eyes.

I remember, for instance, the first time I went to the great palace of Versailles outside Paris and how, as I wandered around among all those gardens and fountains and statues, I had a sense that the place was alive with ghosts which I was just barely unable to see, that somewhere just beneath the surface of all that was going on around me at that moment, the past was going on around me too with such reality and such poignance that I had to have somebody else to tell about it if only to reassure myself that I wasn't losing my mind. I wanted and sorely needed to name to another human being the sights that I was seeing and the thoughts and feelings they were giving rise to. I thought that in a way I could not even surely know what I was seeing physically until I could speak of it to someone else, could not come to terms with what I was feeling as either real or unreal until I could put it into words and speak those words and hear other words in response to mine. But there was nobody to speak to, as it happened, and I can still remember the frustration of it: the sense I had of something trying to be born in me that could not be born without the midwifery of expressing it; the sense, it might not be too much to say, of my self trying to be born, of a threshold I had to cross in order to move on into the next room of who I had it in me just then to become. "In the beginning was the Word," John writes, and perhaps part of what that means is that until there is a word, there can be no beginning.

There are all sorts of theories about how language originated. One of them has it that it originated with people trying to imitate such sounds in nature as the crashing of thunder or the whistling of wind, the meowing of cats or the twittering of birds. Another holds that it started with the kind of interjectory sounds people make when they experience intense sensations, sounds that gradually come to mean either the sensation itself or whatever it was that caused the sensation. Still others, it seems, have advanced the suggestion that language originated from work songs, the kind of chants or rhythmic patterns of grunts or gasps that people are apt to fall into when joined together in some taxing communal enterprise like hunting or building, just as children playing in a sandbox will fall into a kind of sing-song. For all I know there may be some measure of truth in all these theories and in others like them, but what bothers me about them is that they don't go into the mystery deeply enough. Why do people want to name things to each other? What is the impulse out of which the impulse to speak arises?

On the grounds of no scholarly knowledge of the subject at all, I would like to advance still another view of the origin of language, one based on the notion that life itself is a kind of traveling, of seeing the sights. And the more sights you see, the more feelings and thoughts those sights call up in you, the more alive you become to what is going on in the world both around you and inside you, then the more profoundly you need to put a word to it. This word serves many functions. It makes what you see and feel manageable. It provides you with a name to get hold of it by. It gives it a shape and texture with which to distinguish it from all the other things you are seeing and feeling. Beyond that, the word makes it possible to share what you are seeing and feeling with another, to check your view of what is real or strange or beautiful or frightening against another's view. And beyond that there is something else which it seems to me lies very close to the heart of the matter, and that is that in some important sense the thing you are seeing or feeling doesn't even fully exist for you until you have given a word to it. It is not that you feel a pain and then cry out, but that until you cry out, you have not fully lived the pain; that the crying out is not just a symbol of the pain but the part of the pain it becomes yours by and human by. It is not that you feel love and then say "I love you," but that until you say "I love you," you have not fully loved because it is the essence of love as it is also the essence of fear, anger, grief, joy and so on to speak itself—to make itself heard and to make itself hearers.

Or take even the most basic object-words. Until you can look at what is rising in the morning sky and say "sun," or at what is growing on the tree and say "apple," or at the stranger and say "you"—until you can address the world, you cannot fully know the world because knowing fully means not just knowing about but entering into relation with. One thinks here of how in Genesis when God says that it is not good for Adam to be alone and makes helpers for him by forming every beast of the field and bird of the air, he then brings them to him "to see what he would call them." One by one Adam gives them names, and then God makes Eve, and Adam says, "She shall be called woman," thereby giving her a name too because it is not until he can address her that she can be truly his or he can be truly hers. Until we can speak each other's name, we remain in some basic ways strangers to each other just as until we can put names to the sights we see, they too remain strange. Thus, for whatever it's worth, it seems to me that language originates ultimately from humanity's profound sense of inner solitude and isolation out of which words rise up as expressions of humanity's profoundest need, which is the need for community, the need to know and be known, the need to share our lives with one another and with the things of the world because otherwise our life would not be human life.

Child. Star. Rain. Death. Cloud. You. This. My guess is

that at some distant time in the evolution of humankind our ancestors ceased being merely humanoid and became human precisely by fashioning such words as those in their deep solitude, just as they scratched drawings on the walls of their deep caves to give graphic shape to what they had seen on their travels. They spoke words so that they might be heard and answered. Grunting and gasping at their labors, mimicking the cry of birds, crying out in grief and joy, they put words to the things they felt and saw because without the words, without the objectifying, the delimiting, the participating—without, above all, the sharing that words make possible—they could not truly see them or know what they were seeing. "And God said, 'Let there be light'; and there was light." There was no light until God called it into being by naming it. And insofar as this is true for us too —there is no world for us until we can name the world— words are in a way our godly sharing in the work of creation, and the speaking and writing of words is at once the most human and the most holy business we engage in.

Then grammar—that dull word that summons up the dullness of parsing and rules and memorizing but that points to what must have been the next great step in the evolution of language. Words get lonely the way people get lonely. Words hunger for relationship with their kind the way people do. Words need to orient themselves in space and time the way people do too, and the power that resides in words, like the power that resides in the people who use them, is a power that cries out to be harnessed and directed to some end. So tenses are born, and the primitive *is*—the star is, the cloud is, my pain or my joy is— becomes also *was* and *will be,* becomes eventually even *might have been* and *will have been* and *could be yet.* How vast a leap it must have taken, how staggering an extension of the human spirit it must have involved, when some man or woman, standing in some drought-parched stubble, for the first time said not *rain is* because there was no rain there to name but *will rain,* naming the thing that was not but would be; or seeing an empty place by the fire said not *death is* because everybody there around the fire was alive but *death was,* and hence the empty place both by the fire and in the heart.

With *was* and *will be,* humans took their place both within time and also beyond time, being able at last to stand within today and yet also to remember yesterday and anticipate tomorrow in ways that the animals presumably cannot because they are trapped in the cage of *today* with their only time as *now* time because, unlike us, they have no word to bring another time into being. And with time, of course—for us—hope becomes possible and new kinds of fear and longing, all of them to be named into existence like Adam naming the parrot, the antelope; and memory becomes possible and regret and new kinds of sweetness and bitterness, and the past becomes a chart to give us bearings just as the future becomes a magic barrel to give us, in addition to the life we live today, all the lives we may choose to live or not to live tomorrow.

And with terms like *when* and *if* and *therefore* words came into relationship with one another, and it is no longer just "the child dies, the man weeps," but *"because* the child dies, the man weeps," or *"although* the man weeps, the child dies"; and thought becomes possible— understanding, wonder, bewilderment, despair all become possible. Then finally *why,* rising on the horizon like a new and terrible sun both to burn and to illumine. The child dies. The man weeps. The rain comes. Why? With *why* humanity is addressing no longer just the world but is addressing finally whatever or whoever, if anything or anybody, holds the world in existence and causes what *is* to *be*. The ultimate purpose of language, I suspect, is that humanity may speak to God.

With words and grammar, people start speaking in sentences, and there is no longer any limit to what they can and will say. It is important to speak now of the danger of words as well as of their glory because with language, as with all the great extensions of human ingenuity and power and spirit, there is a dark as well as a light side, a curse as well as a blessing. One thinks of Genesis again and of the serpent's saying to Eve that if she ate of the forbidden fruit, her eyes would be opened and she would be like God, knowing good and evil. They are fateful words indeed, and it is testimony to the serpent's cunning that he makes them sound like a promise when they are also, of course, a threat. To name a thing is to know it in a new and powerful way, is to enter into relationship with it, to participate in it, in a sense to bring it into being, and for that very reason, let us who name things beware because some of the things we name are dark and terrible. "In the day that you eat of the forbidden tree," God tells Adam, "you shall die," and that is a way of stating the crux of it.

"In the day that you eat of the forbidden tree," God might have said, "you shall also live" because to be able to stand back from your life enough to name the richness of it is to come for the first time richly alive. But "you shall die" is the shadow side of it because to be able to name death not just as a biological event the way in a sense even the beast names it with a yelp of terror as the slaughterer's knife slits its throat but as a future inevitability is by that very token to die a little already in advance. To give a word to death is to invest it with the power to cast its shadow backward in time. It is to see the future as not just the opening of many doors but as their final closing too. It is to understand that death puts an end not only to the capacity of the body to move through the world but to the capacity of the spirit to move above the world by naming it. Thus death becomes for us what it cannot be for other creatures: not just an end but an unspeakable affront to the very essence of what we are, a terrible grief, a constant unease which it is both life-diminishing to contemplate and yet also life-diminishing to ignore since our knowledge of life's preciousness is closely bound up with our knowledge of life's finitude.

For human beings to come to *know* in the way that words make possible—to eat of the tree of knowledge—is to bring into the world along with death all the other great shadows of hate, doubt, despair, anxiety, and finally evil—which only we can name and of which, among all the creatures of the earth, only we are capable. By calling the others the "dumb" beasts, we rightly single out their inability to speak words as the one characteristic above all others which most crucially distinguishes them from ourselves, and of which their innocence most basically consists. Unlike us, who can be any damned thing or any blessed thing within our range, the dog, the tiger, the sparrow know no other way of being apart from the way they were born to be because they can name no other way; and to contemplate them in their dumbness, their touching and eloquent wordlessness, is to recognize not only what as humans we have immeasurably gained by our ability to speak but also what we have immeasurably lost.

But if the possibility of evil is the greatest danger that our ability to use words involves us in, it is by no means the only one. Like any other symbol, a word not only stands for something else but has in it also some of the power of the thing it stands for. To put into words our anger, our love, our forgiveness, our desire, is, even if we were never to act upon our words, to affect powerfully both the lives of the ones we are addressing and our own lives. We cannot hear the name of the one we love named without our hearts quickening or the name of the thing we dread without our hearts sinking. Words are dangerous because for better or worse they are so powerful, and yet at the same time they are dangerous because they are so weak. They are weak in the sense that, for all their power, they can never say all that there is to say about anything, and the danger is that we are perpetually inclined to forget that.

Not long ago I listened to an astrophysicist talk fascinatingly about the extraordinary strides science has made in understanding such things as the origin of the universe, the nature of matter, the relationship of space to time, and he spoke with such conviction and authority that I found myself asking him finally if he could conceive of a time, maybe a hundred years hence, when all his answers to these great questions might look as primitive and inadequate as the theories of, say, medical science a hundred years ago look to us now. His reply was unabashed. He said that as far as he was concerned, these answers that modern science has reached are final answers, and all we need now is time and money enough to continue research into their ramifications and implications. Nobody could be less qualified than I am to pass judgment on the findings of science at any level, but because I know that, like all answers, these scientific answers are expressed in words and in numbers, which I take to be only another form of words, I simply cannot believe them to be final. It is as impossible for me to believe that the words even of scientific genius can say all there is to say about the origin of the universe as it is impossible for me to believe that the words even of Sophocles or Shakespeare can say all there is to say about human tragedy or the words even of Jesus Christ can say all there is to say about God and about our lives under God. Part, at least, of what I believe the New Testament means by calling Jesus himself the Word of God is that in the final analysis not even the most authentic and inspired words he ever spoke could exhaust the mystery he came to reveal, and that when he proclaimed not "What I say is the truth" but, instead, "I am the truth," he meant, among other things, that the truth cannot be fully caught in any expression of the truth in words but only in the great eloquence and complexity and simplicity of his own life.

Lastly there is the danger of words implicit in their power not just to convey information—"that is a child," "the rain will come"—but also to convey feelings in the sense not just of naming them but of in some measure transmitting them. If it is in any way true that language originates out of our deep inner solitude and our need to escape that solitude by relating ourselves to the world outside the lonely worlds we are within ourselves, then it is not enough merely to tell the world out there who we are but we must also tell what it feels like to be who we are. It is not enough for us merely to tell somebody else that we are happy, say, because in order to share that experience fully, we must enable others to experience it too. We are not content merely to name what is going on inside ourselves but seek to use words that to a degree enable others to feel what it is like to live inside our skins themselves. Then they will really know.

When it comes to spoken words, there are all sorts of auxiliary ways of doing this, of course—the tone of voice, facial expression, gesture and all the non-verbal sounds we make to convey something much richer and more compelling than mere intellectual meaning. And when it comes to conveying this same richness through the written word, there are needless to say a great many other devices to replace these nonverbal ones, as no one knew better, for instance, than such a great prose stylist as John Donne. Listen to a brief passage from one of his sermons.

> David knew he could not retire himself from God in his bedchamber; guards and ushers could not keep him out. He knew he could not defend himself from God in his army; for the Lord of hosts is the Lord of his hosts. If he fled to the Sea, to Heaven, to Hell, he was sure to meet God there; and there thou shalt meet him too, if thou fly from God to the relief of outward comforts, of music, of mirth, of drink, of cordials, of comedies, of conversation. Not that such recreations are unlawful; the mind hath her physic as well as the body; but when thy sadness proceeds from a sense of sin (which is God's key to the door of his mercy, put into thy hand) it is a new and greater sin to go about to overcome that holy sadness with these profane diversions; to fly *ad consolatiunculas creaturalae . . .* to the little and contemptible comforts of little and contemptible creatures. . . . David could not drown his adultery in blood; never think to drown

thine in wine. The ministers of God are suns of thunder, trampling of horses, and runnings of chariots; and if these voices of these ministers cannot overcome thy music, thy security, yet the Angel's trumpet will; . . . that *ite maledicti,* go you accursed into Hell fire is a base that drowns us all. There is no recourse but to God, no relief but in God; and therefore David applied himself to the right method, to make his first access to God.*

As far as the plain sense, the information, of what Donne is trying to convey is concerned, he sums it up well in his last sentence—"There is no recourse but to God, no relief but in God"—but what else does he manage to convey to us with his words, and what devices does he use for conveying it? The "what else" is of course no less than his whole set of complex feelings about this God he is preaching and about the ways in which we are both drawn to him and try to escape him too. Of the devices he uses to convey this complex and ultimately unverbalizable feeling, perhaps the most important is metaphor. Donne speaks of God as the general of a great army, as the inescapable tenant of the Sea, Heaven, Hell, as the custodian of a rich treasure house of mercy to which our sense of sin is the key. In all of this Donne is concerned not so much with illumining our understanding as with enchanting us as he himself is enchanted, with transmitting to us something of his own inner sense of the mystery and majesty of God which in the last analysis words cannot name directly any more than to a blind man words can name directly objects of sight. The sun is like the calling of

---

*John Donne, *Donne's Sermons, Selected Passages* (New York: Oxford University Press, 1919), p. 152.

trumpets, the color green is like the smell of rain, we say
to the blind man; and to one who cannot see as Donne
sees, cannot feel as Donne feels, Donne says God is like
this, God is like that, until we begin to connect his metaphors like points on a graph and come out with a richer
sense of the reality of Donne's experience of God than
could ever be directly named.

All the other devices are in a way related to metaphor
—like the rhythm, for instance. "God's key to the door of
his mercy, put into thy hand," he says, with the rising
iambic pulse, the little catch of breath or caesura after
"mercy" which makes us catch our own breath. The mercy
of God is like that, Donne suggests, that hopeful sound
and beat, that startled little jolt. And there is the allitera-
tion: "thy sadness proceeds from a sense of sin," he says,
with the music of the *s*'s whispering to us as sins and
sadness whisper. We fly from God, he says, to the relief
"of music, of mirth, of cordials, of comedies, of conversa-
tion," using all those *m*'s and *c*'s to tinkle in our ears, as
in a way all these external sources of comfort are themselves at best a kind of tinkling to keep the dark at bay.
And there is assonance: "suns of thunder," "falls of waters," "never think thou to drown thine in wine" as if,
when all else fails, he sings to us for the sake of what the
music of a song can convey beyond the words of it in a way
that reminds us of his great meditation on death where he
says, "Never send to know for whom the bell tolls, it tolls
for thee," so that the relentless and unbroken knell of all
those monosyllables and the changes he rings on the sound
of *o*—to, know, whom, tolls, tolls—begin to ring in our
ears, and more than our ears, like the massive bell itself.

And finally there are the words themselves that he

uses, words thought of now not simply in terms of what the dictionary says they mean but in terms of their shape and color and weight and texture apart from meaning, in terms of what happens when they are oddly and unexpectedly paired. It is a new and greater sin, he says, "to overcome that holy sadness with these profane diversions," and the juxtaposition of "holy" and "sadness" enables those two words to say in tandem what neither of them could say apart, to jolt us into hearing a facet of sadness (its holiness) and a facet of holiness (its sadness) in a more vivid and meaningful way than could be achieved by a whole paragraph of theological exposition. And there is the latinate stateliness and elegance of phrases like "profane diversion," "contemptible comforts," together with Donne's use of Latin itself—his *ad consolatiunculas creaturalae,* his *ite maledicti*—all of which convey an almost architectural sense of the gravity and grandeur of what he is saying, a classic temple of language against an arching sky.

By such devices such as these, words, both written ones and spoken ones, have the power actually to transmit feeling from one person to another, and the rabble-rousing speech, the tear-jerking sermon, scare tactics and so on all bear witness to how dangerous a power that can be, and yet of course it is by virtue of that same power of words that great literature is born with its capacity for not merely transmitting to us—with greater depth, richness and intensity than we are apt to encounter anywhere else—what it is to be human but for actually empowering us in some measure to become more human ourselves.

In his autobiography, Anthony Trollope says this about himself as a writer:

I have always desired to "hew out some lump of earth," and to make men and women walk upon it just as they do walk here among us—with not more of excellence, nor with exaggerated baseness—so that my readers might recognize human beings like to themselves, and not feel themselves to be carried away among gods or demons. If I could do this, then I thought I might succeed in impregnating the mind of the novel-reader with a feeling that honesty is the best policy; that truth prevails while falsehood fails; that a girl will be loved as she is pure, and sweet, and unselfish; that a man will be honored as he is true, and honest, and brave of heart; that things meanly done are ugly and odious, and things nobly done beautiful and gracious. . . . There are many who would laugh at the idea of a novelist teaching either virtue or nobility—those, for instance, who regard the reading of novels as a sin, and those who think it to be simply a pastime. They look upon the tellers of stories as among the tribe of those who pander to the wicked pleasures of a wicked world. I have regarded my art from so different a point of view that I have ever thought of myself as a preacher of sermons, and my pulpit as one which I could make both salutary and agreeable to my audience. I do believe that no girl has arisen from the reading of my pages less modest than she was before, and some may have learned from them that modesty is a charm well worth preserving. I think that no youth has been taught that in falseness and flashness is to be found the road to manliness; but some may have learned from me that it is to be found in truth and a gentle spirit.*

Words like Trollope's are in many ways out of fashion now. To speak of women as pure, sweet, unselfish and to be loved, and of men as true, honest, brave of heart and

---

*Anthony Trollope, *An Autobiography* (New York: Oxford University Press), pp. 125–126.

to be honored smacks of a view of things that we no longer find palatable. For a novelist to speak of himself as a preacher of sermons puts everybody off. But when Trollope—than whom I believe there is no greater novelist in English—says that the calling of a writer is to teach virtue and nobility, and when he expresses the hope that people will learn from his words that true manliness, true humanness, is to be found not in falseness and flashness but in truth and a gentle spirit, that is something else again.

The truth of it seems to be that it is not only that literature contains metaphors but that literature essentially *is* metaphor. Writers travel through life like the rest of us, seeing the sights and responding to them in all sorts of inner ways, and then, like the rest of us, they need, in their loneliness, to put it into words. Like God saying "Let there be light" so that by naming it he can bring it into being, the writers of literature say "Let there be *this*"—this putting into words of their experience of life—so that it can more fully and effectively *be* both for themselves and for the rest of us.

In a letter to a friend about *The Brothers Karamazov*, Dostoevsky wrote, "The chief problem dealt with throughout this particular work is the very one which has, my whole life long, tormented my conscious or subconscious being: the question of the existence of God." Clearly the question was not an academic one for Dostoevsky but a question that arose out of what he calls his tormenting experience, and to put that experience into words he did on a far larger scale what Shakespeare, for instance, did when he wrote "How like a winter hath my absence been from thee." My experience of God and of no-God, Dostoevsky says, is like . . . and then the whole

complex structure and treasury of *The Brothers Karamazov*
comes forth as a single metaphor which enables us to
participate in the depths of that experience as no academic
disquisition could ever do.

And what is the effect upon us, as readers, of sharing
that experience? In what way and to what end does that
work of literature speak to our lives out of Dostoevsky's
life? The book could hardly be less didactic in any narrow
sense. It is full of darkness and ambiguity. The characters
are continually lacerating themselves and each other
through their terrible pride. Ivan's devastating attack on
belief in an all-powerful and loving God nearly overwhelms us as it nearly overwhelms his brother Alyosha,
and Alyosha himself, whose whole life is supposed to
speak for the defense, is in many ways the least convincing
character in the book. It teaches no easy lesson about
virtue and nobility, and yet to read it as seriously as it asks
to be read, and as it was written, is to emerge from it in
some profound way the better for it in the sense of closer
to that truth and gentleness of spirit that Trollope names.
And so it is, I think, with any work of literature that is
worth the time it takes to read it.

If literature is a metaphor for the writer's experience,
a mirror in which that experience is at least partially reflected, it is at the same time a mirror in which the reader
can also see his or her experience reflected in a new and
potentially transforming way. This is what it is like to
search for God in a world where cruelty and pain hide
God, Dostoevsky says—"How like a winter hath my absence been from thee"; how like seeing a poor woman in
a dream with a starving child at her breast; how like Father
Zossima kneeling down at the feet of Dmitri Karamazov

because he sees that great suffering is in store for him and because he knows, as John Donne did, that suffering is holy. And you and I, his readers, come away from our reading with no more proof of the existence or nonexistence of God than we had before, with no particular moral or message to frame on the wall, but empowered by a new sense of the depths of love and pity and hope that is transmitted to us through Dostoevski's powerful words.

Words written fifty years ago, a hundred years ago, a thousand years ago, can have as much of this power today as ever they had it then to come alive for us and in us and to make us more alive within ourselves. That, I suppose, is the final mystery as well as the final power of words: that not even across great distances of time and space do they ever lose their capacity for becoming incarnate. And when these words tell of virtue and nobility, when they move us closer to that truth and gentleness of spirit by which we become fully human, the reading of them is sacramental; and a library is as holy a place as any temple is holy because through the words which are treasured in it the Word itself becomes flesh again and again and dwells among us and within us, full of grace and truth.

18. All's Lost — All's Found

"How my mind has changed in the last decade" is the subject to which I was invited to address myself several years ago, and since the invitation seemed to offer a certain amount of leeway, I undertook to produce less of a formal essay than a few rather informal paragraphs under three different headings. To begin with, *How my mind has changed about myself.*

My readings in Buddhism have long since convinced me that when I talk about myself, I don't really know what I'm talking about. "How do I learn to control myself? To understand myself? To live with myself?" the harried Occidental goes to the Buddhist monk to inquire, and after twenty minutes or so of properly inscrutable silence, the monk says something like, "Show me this self you're fretting about. Then maybe I can help you with it." Needless to say, the point seems to be that when you come right down to it, there's nothing to show. I do not have a self. I am a self. As soon as I draw back to scrutinize "it," I have by the very act of drawing back removed from my scrutiny the very thing I seek to know. So instead of trying to talk about who I am, let me simply describe something of what it feels like to live inside my skin now as compared with ten years ago.

In many ways it feels much the same. As much in my fifties as in my forties, I feel much of the time like a child. I get excited about the kinds of things that excite a ten-year-old. The first snow of the year, for instance. The smell of breakfast. Buying things, especially books, which, like a child, it is less important for me to read than simply to have. Getting things in the mail. Going to the movies. Having somebody remember my name. Remembering somebody's name. Making a decent forehand in tennis. Being praised. Chocolate ice cream. And so on.

Like a child too I feel uneasy in the presence of people who are more grown-up than I am. I find myself saying to them less what I really feel like saying than what I feel they'd like to have me say. When people are taking me seriously as a grown-up—listening to me lecture or preach or talking to me about one of my books—I think to myself *if they only knew.* If someone were to wake me up in the middle of the night with a flashlight in my eyes and, before I had time to think, ask me who I was, I would not say my grown-up name but my childhood name. If they asked my age, I would say not fifty-six but twenty-six. Maybe even sixteen. Given the choice between having flying saucers, the Loch Ness monster, ghosts, magic and miracles generally proven either true or false, I would choose them to be true without a moment's hesitation. And so on again.

The child in me is very much alive, in other words, and though this involves certain serious disadvantages, I would not have it otherwise. A child is apt to see certain things better than his elders, I think, because, less sure than they of what to *expect,* he is more apt than they to see what, actually though unexpectedly, *is*. By the same token, a child is apt to feel certain things more than his elders too because he is not as good as they at keeping his feelings under control, and even though this makes him vulnerable to some emotional inanities that maturity is relatively safe from, I still would not have it any other way.

All of this was as true of me ten years ago as it is now, but there have been changes too. One instance of this is the word that during the last ten years I find I've started to use for sighing with. Instead of the traditional *oh dear* or *oh well* or any of those, again and again I hear myself saying *child, child* in a tone of voice that seems to be a sort of weary reproof and yet a kind of lament too. Don't be so foolish the grown-up in me says to the child. Don't make such a fuss. Don't let the world get under your skin so. Keep your guard up more. Stay on an evener keel. Grow up. That is the reproof. The lament, I think, stems from knowing that the reproof will be heeded all too well. Already the child *is* keeping his guard up more, keeping the world at arm's length more, starting to see less, feel less. It is a step toward maturity and as such to be rejoiced in. But it is a step away from something in its way equally precious and as such to be lamented too. *Child, child* . . . I feel a state of being, a dimension of selfhood, coming to an end, and it is proper that it should come to an end so that something richer and wiser and in the long run even holier can take its place. But the end of anything is sad because the end of anything foreshadows the end, finally, of everything. And that final end is death, about which also my mind has changed, and hence the second heading: *How my mind has changed about death*.

Even forty years ago, let alone ten, I knew that like

everybody else I would die someday, and in my mind I had already died many times. I have never had an ache or pain that wasn't fatal or an illness that wasn't terminal. One of the occupational hazards of being a writer of fiction is to have an imagination as overdeveloped as a blacksmith's right arm. Again and again I have watched the doctor pause for a way to break the tragic news to me. I have lain in a hospital room receiving the final visits of friends. I have said goodbye to my wife and children for the last time. I have attended my own funeral.

There is something to be said for such nonsense. For one thing, to have the doctor tell you that it is not lung cancer after all but just a touch of the flu is in a way to be born again. For another thing, it is to be given back not just your old life again but your old life with a new sense of its pricelessness. At least for a time old grievances, disappointments, irritations, failures, that had cast a shadow over your days suddenly cease to matter much. You are alive. That's all that matters, and the sheer wonder and grace of it are staggering, the sense of life as gift, and the sense of the pricelessness of each moment too, even the most humdrum. The taste of fresh bread. The trip to pick up the laundry. The walk with a friend. They were nearly taken away for good. Someday they will be taken away for good indeed. But in the meantime they are yours. Treasure them for what they will not be forever. Treasure them for what, except by God's grace, they might never have been at all.

All of this was part of what it was like to be me in the 1970s and continues to be so in the 1980s, but at some point during the intervening decade I experienced death in a new way still. I tried to describe the experience in a novel once. There is a scene in which a man goes to visit his sister Miriam's grave in a Brooklyn cemetery. He tries to shed a tear for her, but the tear won't come. Instead, his mind begins to wander until in a sense it wanders off altogether, and he ends up just staring down at the grass so hard that he doesn't even see it. He doesn't have a thought in his head. What follows next he describes like this:

> I was still standing there in this kind of empty-headed trance, and then it was like what happens when, just as you're about to go to sleep at night, you seem to trip over something and can feel the whole bed shake under you. I *came to,* I suppose you would say. Some stirring in the air or quick movement of squirrel or bird brought me back to myself, and just at that instant of being brought back to myself, I knew that the self I'd been brought back to was some fine day going to be as dead as Miriam. I knew it not just in the usual sense of knowing it but knew it in almost the Biblical sense of having sex with it. I knew I didn't just *have* a body. I *was* a body. It was like walking into a closed door at night. The thud of it jolted me down to the roots of my hair.
>
> The body I was was going to be dead. I'd known it before, but here I banged right into it—not a lesson this time but a collision. You might say that there at my sister's grave I finally lost my innocence, saw the unveiling of middle-age's last and most intimate secret. There in Brooklyn I was screwed by my own death.*

At some point during the last ten years, in other words, I came, like the narrator in the novel, to know my death in a new way. What I had feared as a hypochondriac came

---

*Frederick Buechner, *The Book of Bebb* (New York: Atheneum, 1979), pp. 197–198.

to seem, by comparison, a small thing or, more accurately, a constellation of small things. I had feared the pain and indignity of disease. I had feared hospitals—the smell, the sterility, the depersonalization. I had dreaded the last farewells. I had dreaded leaving the party while I was still having a good time. I had feared and dreaded the ultimate separation from everything and everybody I held most dear. But behind all these fears, and essential to their fearsomeness, was the presupposition that the self that I am would be in some sense around to experience them, down to and including my own funeral.

What I have come to experience since, and with a degree of immediacy impossible to describe, is the extinction of the self itself. With something more than my imagination I have come at odd moments to experience something more than my death, that is to say something more than my death as an event in which my self will participate. I have come to experience it as a nonevent which I will no longer have or be a self to participate in it with. Call it Nothingness. Call it the End. And the curious thing is that when it comes to this most staggering reality of all, I am no longer afraid.

Dying and dissolution continue to strike fear in me. Death itself does not. Ten years ago if somebody had offered me a vigorous, healthy life that would never end, I would have said yes. Today I think I would say no. I love my life as much as I ever did and will cling on to it for as long as I can, but life without death has become as unthinkable to me as day without night or waking without sleep. Which brings me to the third and final heading, which is *How my mind has changed about God.*

Needless to say this is closely related to the other two.

The child in me must die so the man in me can be born. Yet the man in me must die too, all of me, the most that I have it in my power to become as well as the least out of whose demise the most emerges. And yet timorous, overimaginative, doom-ridden, life-loving, self-serving and self-centered and sinful as I am, I find that I contemplate this fact with a new and curious absence of fear. Why should this be so?

By way of an answer I find myself drawing again from a novel of mine called *Godric*. It has to do with a medieval hermit-saint who for many years chastened his flesh in the icy waters of the river Wear near the city of Durham in northern England. As a very old man he describes the experience of bathing in it in the dead of winter:

> First there's the fiery sting of cold that almost stops my breath, the aching torment in my limbs. I think I may go mad, my wits so outraged that they seek to flee my skull like rats a ship that's going down. I puff. I gasp. Then inch by inch a blessed numbness comes. I have no legs, no arms. My very heart grows still. These floating hands are not my hands. The ancient flesh I wear is rags for all I feel of it.
>
> "Praise, praise!" I croak. Praise God for all that's holy, cold, and dark. Praise him for all we lose, for all the river of the years bears off. Praise him for stillness in the wake of pain. Praise him for emptiness. And as you race to spill into the sea, praise him yourself, old Wear. Praise him for dying and the peace of death.
>
> In the little church I built of wood for Mary, I hollowed out a place for him. Perkin brings him by the pail and pours him in. Now that I can hardly walk, I crawl to meet him there. He takes me in his chilly lap to wash me of my sins. Or I kneel down beside him till within his depths I see a star.

Sometimes this star is still. Sometimes she dances. She is Mary's star. Within that little pool of Wear she winks at me. I wink at her. The secret that we share I cannot tell in full. But this much I will tell. What's lost is nothing to what's found, and all the death that ever was, set next to life, would scarcely fill a cup.*

At the age of one hundred the old man knows what at my age I am only just beginning to see—that if it is by grace we are saved, it is by grace too that we are lost, or lost at least in the sense of losing our selves, our lives, our all. In the past, when my faith was strong, I always trusted God more or less. I trusted him with my life, which is to say I trusted him but with the presupposition that I would always be in some measure alive to say to him in the words of the *Te Deum*, "Oh Lord, in thee have I trusted; let me never be confounded," in the sense that I would always be around to cajole with him, plead with him, and in general to remind him to be the God of mercy and love I always trusted him to be. The change is that now I begin, at least, to trust him with my death. I begin, at least, to see that death is not merely a biological necessity but a necessity too in terms of the mystery of salvation.

We find by losing. We hold fast by letting go. We become something new by ceasing to be something old. This seems to be close to the heart of that mystery. I know no more now than I ever did about the far side of death as the last letting-go of all, but I begin to know that I do not need to know and that I do not need to be afraid of not knowing. God knows. That is all that matters.

_____
*Frederick Buechner, *Godric* (New York: Atheneum, 1980; Harper & Row, 1983), pp. 95–96.

Out of Nothing he creates Something. Out of the End he creates the Beginning. Out of selfness we grow, by his grace, toward selflessness, and out of that final selflessness, which is the loss of self altogether, "eye hath not seen nor ear heard, neither have entered into the heart of man" what new marvels he will bring to pass next. All's lost. All's found. And if such words sound childish, so be it. Out of each old self that dies some precious essence is preserved for the new self that is born; and within the child-self that is part of us all, there is perhaps nothing more precious than the fathomless capacity to trust.